Delville Wood on the Somme was the most famous battle ever fought by South Africans. Through this action other nations learnt to respect the fighting qualities of the men from the fledgling Union of South Africa. Erstwhile foes, Boer and Briton, fought shoulder to shoulder against the pride of the German Army. They withstood waves of attacking infantrymen; were subjected to savage artillery fire which reached a crescendo of seven shells a second, pulverising the wood and obliterating the defences; then fought hand-to-hand until overrun; threw back the enemy; and fought on with unbelievable tenacity.

The bone-weary survivors defended the wood through five days and six nights of hell, eventually being forced into a corner of the wood. The orders were to hold on at all costs – and this they did despite appalling casualties. The saga of Delville Wood will never be forgotten by South Africa, yet the story of the battle, told through the eyes of the participants was never fully documented – accounts read like fiction, yet are wholly true.

We learn about youngsters from the plains of Southern Africa who earned the admiration of their enemy. After being shelled for eight hours they stood up from the mud to repel fresh assaults. We read of the Victoria Cross won through rescuing a wounded officer under fire; a man blown up and buried who continued on to deliver his message and earn the DCM; the officer who was captured then knocked out his guard to return to the fighting; the colonel who fought like a private with rifle and mills bombs; and many more.

The Germans' experiences are also chronicled. Extracts from their regimental histories paint a picture of their dogged determination to retake the wood. Their order was that the enemy was not to advance except over corpses! The author interviewed many of the South African survivors, now long gone, and has visited the wood on many occasions during the past thirty-three years. The trilogy of books he wrote on the battle has been combined into a riveting account of 'the bloodiest battle hell of 1916'.

In 1917 *The Times* of London recounted, 'No battlefield on all the Western Front was more bitterly contested than was "Devil's Wood" … [where] South African forces won their imperishable fame – grimly hanging on against overwhelming odds and repulsing counter attacks by troops five and six times their number.'

Ian Uys inherited his love of military history from his father, Jack (1910-59). During his schooldays in Uitenhage he wrote to an encyclopedia for the names of all South African VC winners. He was sent three names, yet at the time he knew of 25!

He volunteered for and served in the SA Air Force Gymnasium in 1960, then attended the University of Cape Town and graduated B Commerce. Uys captained the UCT Boxing team and was selected as South Africa's first AIESEC commerce student to work in the USA and Australia. After marrying Barbara Bowers, a former Londoner, he qualified as a chartered accountant then lived in England where he did further VC research.

In 1973 he wrote and published *For Valour*, the history of Southern Africa's Victoria Cross Heroes. It has a natural successor in *Enduring Valour* as it updates the records of valour by South Africans. Uys has been interested in the personal reminiscences of personalities caught up in military history and has written many books about them.

He served in the Heidelberg Commando in the seventies. In 1977 he was a platoon commander in the operational area and was awarded the De Wet Decoration. In 1989 he ran for parliament as a Democratic Party candidate for Germiston District, a strong National Party ward. Though he lost, he believes that in a small way it contributed to the change in the country the following year.

Uys is a practising auditor in Knysna and has three children and four grandchildren. He is a former chairman of the SA Military History Society, has completed ten Comrades' Marathons of 90km and was a private pilot for many years. He has developed his family's Bushman Valley Resort near Prince Albert and is a keen nature conservationist.

Hold At All Costs!

The Epic Battle of Deville Wood 1916

Ian Uys

 Helion & Company Limited

Helion & Company Limited
26 Willow Road
Solihull
West Midlands
B91 1UE
England
Tel. 0121 705 3393
Fax 0121 711 4075
Email: info@helion.co.uk
Website: www.helion.co.uk
Twitter: @helionbooks
Visit our blog http://blog.helion.co.uk/

Published by Helion & Company 2015

Designed and typeset by Bookcraft Ltd, Stroud, Gloucestershire
Cover designed by Euan Carter, Leicester (www.euancarter.com)
Printed by Gutenberg Press Limited, Tarxien, Malta

Text © Ian Uys 2015
Images © as individually credited

ISBN 978-1-910294-37-6

British Library Cataloguing-in-Publication Data.
A catalogue record for this book is available from the British Library.

For details of other military history titles published by Helion & Company
Limited contact the above address, or visit our website: http://www.helion.co.uk.

We always welcome receiving book proposals from prospective authors.

Dedicated to:
All mothers, wives, sweethearts and sisters who have watched their
loved ones go off to war.

Hold At All Costs

On 17 July: General Lukin noted how fatigued the men were. By then all his troops had been in action for at least 48 hours.

> On his return to Brigade HQ he discussed the situation on the telephone with General Furse [CO 9th Division}, but could get no hope of relief or reinforcements. General Congreve's [CO XIII Corps] instructions stood that Delville must be held at any cost. [Buchan, p.68]

On 19 July: Captain Claude Brown said:

> I heard Colonel Thackeray tell the men that he would not leave the trench unless relieved, and the men were encouraged to hang on until the very end.

On 20 July: Lieutenant Edward Phillips, although himself wounded, fought on. He later recalled:

> Even when the situation was at a most critical stage, Lieut-Col Thackeray issued orders to hold the line at all costs, and when the men were absolutely beat by fatigue, he went up and down the trenches encouraging the men …

At 1.00pm on 20 July Lieut-Col Thackeray sent a last desperate message to Lukin:

> … I am alone with Phillips who is wounded and only a couple of sergeants. Please relieve these men today without fail as I fear they have come to the end of their endurance.

The insignia of the division, brigade and battalions
(Ditsong National Museum of Military History)

Contents

List of illustrations   vii
List of maps   xiii
Foreword   xiv
Acknowledgements   xvi
Introduction   xviii

1   Moulding the Brigade   21
2   French entrée   41
3   The Big Push   55
4   The Village – 14 July   69
5   The Wood – 15 July   90
6   Fighting escalates – 16 July   106
7   Holding on – 17 July   122
8   The Bombardment – 18 July   128
9   At all Costs – 19-20 July   150
10   Aftermath   165

Appendices

I   Biographies   174
II   An Overview   188
III   Poems   191
IV   German regimental histories   195
V   British Order of Battle   198
VI   1st SA Infantry Brigade   200
VII   Decorations and Mentions   201

Bibliography   206
Index   209

List of Illustrations

The insignia of the division, brigade and battalions (Ditsong National
Museum of Military History) vi

The Late Justice M T Steyn. xiv

The chateau at Longueval. (T Fairgrieves) xv

Irmgard Weisser. xvi

The Kirkman children circa 1904. Back row Sydney 8, Doug 11. Front: Mary
3, Katherine 5, Alfred 13. (P Kirkman) xviii

'Gott mit Uns'- Service held near Flers on 22 June, 1916. (I Weisser) xx

Brig-Gen H T Lukin CMG DSO. (J Buchan) 21

Officers of the 1st SAI Battalion – Cape Regt
Back Row: Capt P J Jowett, Lieut S W E Style, Lieut C B Parsons,
Sec-Lieut W D Henry, Sec-Lieut C W Reid, Capt G J Miller, Lieut E A
Davis. Third Row: Lieut K Keith, Sec-Lieut A W Craig, Sec-Lieut A C
Harrison, Sec-Lieut A H Brown, Capt H H Jenkins, Sec-Lieut L I Isaacs,
Lieut J T Bain, Capt T Ormiston, Lieut E J Burgess, Capt J J Harris,
Capt E Whiting, Lieut W Larmuth, Capt E Burges, Capt T G McEwen.
Second Row: Capt J R Leisk, Capt F H Heal, Capt H Woodhead (Adj),
Lieut-Col F S Dawson (OC), Major J F Purcell DSO, Major R A St
Leger, Capt A C Wearner. Front Row: Sec-Lieut C F Nicholson, Lieut
A W Liefeldt, Lieut T O Priday, Sec-Lieut W S Dent, Sec-Lieut W S
Brown, Lieut C J Bate. (Ditsong National Museum of Military History) 22

Officers of the 2nd SAI Battalion – Natal & OFS Regt. Top Row: Lieut
Pearce, Lieut Lagerwall, Lieut T W Bru de Wold, Lieut Jenkins, Lieut
R Beverley, Lieut Symons, Lieut W J Hill, Capt W Gray, Lieut C T
Letchford, Lieut L Greene. Middle Row: Lieut Turnley, Capt E Barlow,
Lieut R G Miller, Lieut A R Knibbs, Lieut Forrester, Capt E A Legge,
Lieut H E Creed, Capt MacDougal, Capt Symmes, Lieut E V Tatham,
Lieut C L Mulcahy, Capt C R Heenan, Chaplain/Captain C J Walshe,
Lieut Perkins. Seated: Capt W F Hoptroff, Capt Sullivan, Capt F G
Walsh, Major Baker, Lieut-Col W E Tanner (OC), Major Christian, Capt
H W Bamford, Capt H H Gee, Capt H H Clifford. On ground: Lieut B
N MacFarlane, Lieut J E Cochrane. (Victoria Club, Pietermaritzburg) 23

Officers of the 3rd SAI Battalion – Transvaal and Rhodesia. Back Row: Capt Burrough, Lieut H M Hirzel, Capt R R Sharp, Lieut Wilson, Lieut A L Paxton, Lieut H G Elliot, Lieut A E Sharp. Second Row: Lieut O H de B Thomas, Lieut J B Baker, Lieut D M Abel, Lieut Ellis, Lieut E J Phillips, Capt Perrol, Lieut Gardener, Sec-Lieut Bliss, Capt A W H MacDonald, Captain/Dr S Liebson, Lieut H N Healey. Seated: Capt D R McLachlan, Capt Sprenger, Capt Mills, Major Hemming, Major Young, Lieut-Col E F Thackeray (OC), Major Webber, Capt J W Jackson, Capt R F C Medlicott, Capt Montgomery, Capt E V Vivian. Seated on ground: Lieut Rogers, Lieut Thompson, Lieut F W S Burton, Capt L W Tomlinson, Lieut B H L Dougherty. (Ditsong National Museum of Military History) 24

Officers of the 4th SAI Battalion – SA Scottish. Back Row: Sec-Lieut C S Bell, Lieut J Watkins, Lieut Micklem, Lieut J L Shenton, Lieut M L Norton, Lieut A Young VC, Capt F Mitchell, Lieut J French. Middle Row: Lieut J McCubbin, Lieut R D Graham, Lieut H G Oughterson, Lieut R B Thorburn, Lieut C M Guest, Lieut A H Brown, Lieut C Duff, Sec-Lieut A Gemmell, Lieut T Farrell, Lieut A S Taylor, Lieut R D Grierson, Lieut W D Charlton, Lieut H M Newson, Lieut G Smith, Hon Lieut Z B Bayly, Lieut A M Cameron. Front Row: Capt R Anderson, Capt E C Grady, Capt E G Clerk, Capt T H Ross, Capt S Thomson, Major D M Macleod DCM, Lieut-Col F A Jones DSO (OC), Capt C M Browne, Major/Dr M S Power, Major D R Hunt, Capt Morton, Capt G Mowat, Capt G E W Marshall. Absent: Capt S C Russell, Capt H McVeigh, Sec-Lieut C Maclean. (Ditsong National Museum of Military History) 25

On the *Dunvegan Castle*. (J Carstens) 27

Lieut Liefeldt at Mersa Matruh. (C W Reid) 31

Relaxing in the desert. (C W Reid) 33

Private Albert Marr and Jackie. (Ditsong National Museum of Military History) 34

Jack Carstens. (J Carstens) 35

Senussi Arabs under guard. (C W Reid) 36

Front left: L/Cpl Maurice Woolf and friends en route to France on board the *Oriana*. (M Kantey) 37

Iron Cross and presentation case. (P K A Digby) 39

The SA Scottish arrive at Marseilles. (Transvaal Scottish Regimental Museum) 42

Cyril Weldon. (D O'Reilly) 44

Lieut Chauncey Reid. (C W Reid) 45

Walter Giddy. (J Morris) 48

'Bonne chance mon camerade'. (*The War Illustrated* Vol IV)   48

Lieut Fred English. (Robertson Museum)   50

The village square – facing west. (T Fairgrieves)   53

The attack. (*The War Illustrated* Vol V)   57

The attack on Montauban. (*The War Illustrated* Vol V)   59

Lieut W Nimmo Brown. (*South Africa Magazine*)   61

Shellburst. (Ditsong National Museum of Military History)   62

German POW's assisting Tommy stretcher-bearers. (Ditsong National
   Museum of Military History)   64

A shattered German trench and dugout. (Ditsong National Museum of
   Military History)   67

The Longueval town hall and school – pre 1914. (T Fairgrieves)   69

(*The War Illustrated* Vol VII)   73

L/Cpl Joey and Pte Victor Pattison. (Justice K Satchwell)   74

(*The War Illustrated* Vol VI)   76

Boysie Nash. (P Kirkman)   77

(*The War Illustrated* Vol VII)   79

A French village under bombardment. (Ditsong National Museum of Military
   History)   84

Lieut Anno Noack of the German Artillery. (Mrs A Noack)   86

Generalstabschef Erich von Falkenhayn. (I Weisser)   86

Genmaj Grautoff. (IR 26 History)   87

Resting during the march to the Somme – 13 July 1916. (RIR 107 History)   88

Oberst Graf von Wuthenau. (RIR 107 History)   88

(*Deeds that Thrill the Empire*)   90

(*The War Illustrated* Vol VII)   92

Lieut Walter Hill. (Major W Speirs and Mrs D Nel)   93

(*The War Illustrated* Vol VI)   93

(*The War Illustrated* Vol VIII)   94

German troops before an attack. (I Weisser)   99

Entrenched Tommies with Vickers guns. (Ditsong National Museum of
   Military History)   102

The Sugar Factory – Waterlot Farm – pre 1914. (T Fairgrieves)   104

North-west corner. (*The War Illustrated* Vol VI)   107

Pte Mannie Faulds rescuing Lieut Arthur Craig. (Painting by W
   Bagdapopulos in the author's collection)   109

(*Deeds that Thrill the Empire*)   111

An unexploded British shell. (I Weisser)   113

Pte Harry Cooper. (Springbok Sept 1972)   113

Capt/Padre E St C Hill. (St John's High School)   114
A group of German officer prisoners. (Ditsong National Museum of Military
    History)   116
A wounded German soldier. (Ditsong National Museum of Military History)   118
South Delville Wood, north Trônes Wood, Waterlot Farm and trench systems
    on 2 July 1916. (Mrs M van der Westhuizen)   119
(*Deeds that Thrill the Empire*)   123
The Springbokls repelling a counter-attack in Delville Wood. (*The Graphic*)   124
Pte Garnet Tanner in 1914 after the train crash. (A Tanner)   126
Pte Frank Maskew. (D McCarthy)   129
(*The War Illustrated* Vol III)   132
(*Deeds that Thrill the Empire*)   133
Clive Featherstone. (Mrs M Stuckey)   134
Sec-Lieut Arthur Knibbs. (Knibbs family)   134
Reinforcements enter the devastated wood. (Dept of Foreign Affairs and
    Information)   135
(*Deeds that Thrill the Empire*)   137
(*The War Illustrated* Vol VII)   138
Pte Arthur Betteridge early in 1917. (A Betteridge)   138
(*Deeds that Thrill the Empire*)   140
(*The War Illustrated* Vol VI)   143
The IR 26 storming Longueval. (IR 26 History)   148
Major Schönberg. (N Cave)   149
Private C B Stuart. (R Stuart)   150
(*The War Illustrated* Vol VI)   151
(*Deeds that Thrill the Empire*)   152
Major V E Wepener DSO. (History of the ILH)   153
Private L Frank Marillier. (Mrs M Marillier)   155
(*The War Illustrated* Vol VII)   156
German officer POWs alongside blasted concrete bunker being guarded by a
    Jock. (Ditsong National Museum of Military History)   158
(*Deeds that Thrill the Empire*)   159
Major Billy Congreve. (W Congreve: *Armageddon Road, a VC's diary 1914-16*)   160
Private Albert Hill of the Royal Welch Fusiliers winning his VC. (*Deeds that
    Thrill the Empire*)   161
(*The War Illustrated* Vol V)   162
Maurice Cristel aged 91. (*The Star*)   163
(*The War Illustrated* Vol VII)   167
(*Deeds that Thrill the Empire*)   170

L/Cpl William Hewitt VC. (Ditsong National Museum of Military History)   172
Pte William Faulds VC. (Ditsong National Museum of Military History)   176
Lieut Garnet Green MC. (Brian K Thomas)   178
Captain S F Kirkman. (P Kirkman)   179
Arthur Knibbs and his wife. (Knibbs Family)   179
Captain Stephen Liebson. (*South Africa Magazine*)   180
Frank Maskew. (Mrs P McCarthy)   181
Sec-Lieut Joey Pattison. (Justice K Satchwell)   182
Lieutenant Edward Phillips. (Ditsong National Museum of Military History)   182
Joe Samuels, 99, probably the last survivor of Delville Wood, with the author
    on 23 April 1997. (I Uys)   183
Gordon Smith. (E Badenhorst)   184
Tanner brothers: Standing – Stanley and Garnet DCM. Seated Doug MM.
    (A Tanner)   185
Lieut Alex 'Sandy' Young. (*The War Illustrated* Vol VII)   187
A Lewis-gun Team. (Ditsong National Museum of Military History)   189
Painting 'Delville Wood' by Sir William Orpen. (Durban Museum and Art
    Gallery)   193
Delville Wood, October 1918. (Author's collection)   194
Relaxing prisoners. (Ditsong National Museum of Military History)   196
The Distinguished Service Order, Military Cross, Distinguished Conduct
    Medal, Military Medal. (Joslin)   201
A Victoria Cross. (I Uys)   201

List of Maps

The Somme 30 June 1916.   56
Attack on Longueval 14 July 1916. (J Ewing – *The History of the*
    9th Scottish Division)   70
Longueval and Delville Wood – July 1916.   72
The German Brown Line – Braune Stellung – on 13 July 1916.
    (*Army Quarterly* 1925)   82
1st SAI Company dispositions. (I Uys)   97
Delville Wood – Longueval 17-18 July 1916. (Ordnance Survey)   145
German units deployed at Delville Wood 18-19 July 1916.   147

Foreword[1]

The passage of time has the same effect on human events as on flowers. The elements and aspects of an event such as a climactic battle open up, as it were, in due course of time like the unfolding of a flower petal by petal, until the full and true nature thereof finally appears before the eyes of the beholder.

Time has now, after seventy [now 99] years, had this effect on that event of exceptional courage, suffering and devotion to duty known to us as 'the Battle of Delville Wood'. And by also weaving the strands of the German side thereof into the tapestry of that battle Ian Uys has succeeded in singularly effective fashion in this further 'Delville book' to demonstrate that during those fateful days in the high summer of 1916 Longueval and Delville Wood was the fearsome stage upon which a terrible drama of brave suffering and self-sacrifice was enacted by the mostly very young fighting men of the contending sides, that all the participants therein were convinced of the justness of their respective causes and that they were moved by that belief to fight to the death, if necessary, for the preservation and advancement of the values upon which those causes were based.

All those young soldiers confronting and wounding, maiming or killing each other within the splintered confines of the once-beautiful village and wood are now, by the praiseworthy efforts of Mr Uys, seen in fact to have been the 'innocents' mauled or destroyed by a conflict not of their making, into which they were impelled by social and political forces beyond their control.

Probably as many, if not more, young Germans as South Africans still lie unburied where they fell on that battlefield, and time has now blended the remains of those erstwhile enemies in the substance of the re-grown wood, the new trees covering and replacing the divisions and ravages of conflict. As it now stands Delville Wood

The Late Justice M T Steyn.

1   Originally appeared as the Foreword to the author's *Longueval*.

The chateau at Longueval. (T Fairgrieves)

should consequently be seen and treated also as a symbol of reconciliation between the South African and German peoples, and I am confident that this book will materially assist in that being done.

Mr Justice M T Steyn
Chairman of the Delville
Wood Fund Raising Committee
Onze Rust
April 11, 1986

Acknowledgements

During my research into the Battle of Delville Wood I had the honour of interviewing many South African survivors of the battle. In all cases they evinced a deep respect for the fighting qualities of the enemy.

There is very little contemporary English literature covering the German side of the fighting. When Irmgard Weisser, a South African born resident of Germany agreed to translate the relevant extracts from the various German regimental histories she made it possible for this book to be written. I am therefore deeply indebted to her for all the work she did in researching and translating German works.

In addition, her late husband, Arno, is thanked for many of the photographs we have used as illustrations. I am also grateful for the assistance of Paul V Mc Keown of Hamburg, Ilse Krejce and her staff of the public libraries in Villingen and Schwenningen and to Gerhard Buck of the Bibliothek für Zeitgeschichte-Weltkriegsbücherei, Stuttgart.

No historical book can be written without the assistance of many people. I am particularly indebted to the following for their help and advice:

Brigadier D Fourie, Professor of Strategic Studies at the University of South Africa, Col A Malan of Fort Klapperkop, Pretoria, the late Mrs Meg vd Westhuizen, daughter of Col E F Thackeray, the late Mr Brian Tanner, son of Gen W Tanner,

Irmgard Weisser.

Cmdr Mac Bisset, the late Mr Don Forsyth, Major Annette van Jaarsveld, Military Information Bureau, Mr Clemens Doetinchem de Rande, Jill Reid for the use of her father-in-law's diaries, John Morris for the use of his Uncle Walter Giddy's diary, Justice Katherine Satchell for her original research on the Pattison brothers, Peter Kirkman for information about James Nash and the Kirkman brothers, Derek O'Reilly for the correspondence between his late father and Cyril Weldon, Phillida McCarthy for the letters written by her father, Frank Maskew, the staff of the Cape Archives,the SA National Defence Force Documentation Centre, the director and staff of the Ditsong National Museum of Military History, Emile Badenhorst of the Port Elizabeth Bayworld Museum for the letters of Gordon Smith, Vernon Abbott for information about Dave Grindley and to all others who in so many ways made the compilation of this book possible. Cordial thanks are due to the various publishers for permission to quote from works listed in the bibliography.

Introduction

Each year Delville Wood day was remembered – not because this First World War battle played a significant part in the war, but because it represents the bravery, fortitude and self-sacrifice of South African soldiers. It was described by an eminent British military historian, Sir Basil Liddel Hart, as the bloodiest battle-hell of 1916. This was in a year when over a million men were killed in action.

The battle took part in the Somme area of France, in the village of Longueval and its adjoining wood – the *Bois de la Ville* or Wood of the Village. The British attack on a twenty kilometre front had incurred massive casualties, 60,000 on the first day, of whom 20,000 were killed. The South African brigade was in reserve and from 14 July when they were first committed they knew there would be no relief. They had to hold the wood at all costs.

English and Afrikaans speakers fought together. No Blacks were allowed to fight at the time but a number of Coloureds took part. During the next five days the South Africans held the wood despite over 100,000 shells levelling all the trees.

Eventually on the 20th three wounded officers and 140 men were relieved, out of 121 officers and 3,052 men who had taken the wood. They were ordinary South

The Kirkman children circa 1904. Back row Sydney 8, Doug 11. Front: Mary 3, Katherine 5, Alfred 13. (P Kirkman)

Africans who had done an extraordinary thing – and proved to the world that their soldiers were second to none.

The casualty returns sent a shock through the country as many families were affected. The accompanying photograph of the Kirkman children taken in about 1906, is a graphic example. All three boys would take part in the Delville Wood fighting and all became casualties: one killed, one wounded and taken prisoner and the third badly wounded. May such sacrifices never again be demanded of our people.

The capture of Longueval village and the adjacent Delville Wood was a prime objective in the taking of the German second line (the Braune Stellung) at the Somme. The village dominated a ridge which overlooked the allied armies and was the centre of an important road network.

Besides some modernisation, the village is much the same today as it was before the battle. The town square is still a gathering place for its people and fairs there are not uncommon. The people are friendly and in harmony with the lovely Picardy countryside around them.

War has come all too often to this farming region. During the Franco-Prussian War, in August 1870 a French camp was pitched close to the Longueval chateau. The Emperor Napoleon III and his son, the Prince Imperial, were staying at the chateau when it was suddenly shelled by a Prussian horse battery.

In August 1914 the village was occupied by the Germans who set about fortifying it, as it overlooked the front line a few kilometres away. By July 1916 Longueval was virtually impregnable. Tunnels connected house cellars with strong points both in the village and in the adjoining Delville Wood.

It soon became apparent to the allies that the village could not be taken without the wood, nor could the wood be taken unless the village fell. The story of the battle for the village is thus also the story of the fight for the wood. A see-saw battle was to rage for over two months before the allies, with the assistance of tanks, managed to break through.

The Germans generally refer to the enemy as British or English. In Delville Wood until 20 July and in Longueval partly, they were in fact South Africans, which the Germans only discovered after they had taken South African prisoners. They were extremely surprised to find soldiers from such a far country as their opponents. One of the German commanders, Oberst Grautoff, had in fact served in German South West Africa!

The histories of the various British regiments who fought here from July to September 1916 have been available to English-speakers for many years, so I was intrigued to learn more about their erstwhile adversaries.

An entirely new perspective on the battle resulted. It became apparent that the Germans at Longueval and Delville Wood had suffered as much and shown the same heroism as their counterparts in the Allied army. By comparing the experiences of 'the other side', one gains an in-depth insight into the battle.

Although the battle for the village and wood formed a small part of the overall campaign, the fighting its combatants experienced stands second to none.

'Gott mit Uns'- Service held near Flers on 22 June, 1916. (I Weisser)

In order to avoid confusion the South African and British side of the battle is described in each chapter, then the German side. It is therefore possible to read either side's versions as a coherent whole. It is interesting to find how similar their experiences were.

1

Moulding the Brigade

During August 1915 the 1st South African Infantry Brigade was raised and trained at Potchefstroom. Brigadier Henry Timson 'Tim' Lukin CMG DSO, 55, a veteran of the Zulu War of 1879, selected younger men in preference to veterans as he knew that the conditions in France were entirely different from those experienced during the Anglo-Boer War.

Among the notable exceptions were Major Harry Gee, 48, and Lieut Alexander 'Sandy' Young, 43, who had won the VC in the Cape Police during the South African War. Young then served in the Bambata Rebellion of 1906. He was a garrulous Irishman whose blarney may have worn out Lukin's defences. He was also the most outstanding horseman the British army had.

Brig-Gen H T Lukin CMG DSO. (J Buchan)

Other Anglo-Boer war veterans included all the battalion commanders, a former Boer officer, Nicholas Vlok, 49, Sgt-Major James Thomson, 35, and L/Cpl Willie Catton, 39, as well as virtually all the senior officers.

Officers of the 1st SAI Battalion – Cape Regt
Back Row: Capt P J Jowett, Lieut S W E Style, Lieut C B Parsons, Sec-Lieut W D Henry, Sec-Lieut C W Reid, Capt G J Miller, Lieut E A Davis.
Third Row: Lieut K Keith, Sec-Lieut A W Craig, Sec-Lieut A C Harrison, Sec-Lieut A H Brown, Capt H H Jenkins, Sec-Lieut L I Isaacs, Lieut J T Bain, Capt T Ormiston, Lieut E J Burgess, Capt J J Harris, Capt E Whiting, Lieut W Larmuth, Capt E Burges, Capt T G McEwen.
Second Row: Capt J R Leisk, Capt F H Heal, Capt H Woodhead (Adj), Lieut-Col F S Dawson (OC), Major J F Purcell DSO, Major R A St Leger, Capt A C Wearner.
Front Row: Sec-Lieut C F Nicholson, Lieut A W Liefeldt, Lieut T O Priday, Sec-Lieut W S Dent, Sec-Lieut W S Brown, Lieut C J Bate.
(Ditsong National Museum of Military History)

The 1st Battalion comprised units from the Cape and was commanded by Lieut-Col Frederick Dawson, 40, from Brighton. He had served in India, Malaya and the South African War. During the campaign in South West Africa he commanded the 4th SA Mounted Rifles.

The 1st Battalion's four companies were: A from Western Province, B from Eastern Province, C from Kimberley (called the Workers' Company) and D from Cape Town (the Clerical Company).

Officers of the 2nd SAI Battalion – Natal & OFS Regt.
Top Row: Lieut Pearce, Lieut Lagerwall, Lieut T W Bru de Wold, Lieut Jenkins, Lieut R Beverley, Lieut Symons, Lieut W J Hill, Capt W Gray, Lieut C T Letchford, Lieut L Greene.
Middle Row: Lieut Turnley, Capt E Barlow, Lieut R G Miller, Lieut A R Knibbs, Lieut Forrester, Capt E A Legge, Lieut H E Creed, Capt MacDougal, Capt Symmes, Lieut E V Tatham, Lieut C L Mulcahy, Capt C R Heenan, Chaplain/Captain C J Walshe, Lieut Perkins.
Seated: Capt W F Hoptroff, Capt Sullivan, Capt F G Walsh, Major Baker, Lieut-Col W E Tanner (OC), Major Christian, Capt H W Bamford, Capt H H Gee, Capt H H Clifford.
On ground: Lieut B N MacFarlane, Lieut J E Cochrane. (Victoria Club, Pietermaritzburg)

The 2nd Battalion (Natal, Orange Free State and the Border) was commanded by Lieut-Col William Tanner, 40, the only South-African born battalion commander. He had served in the Natal Carbineers, took part in the Defence of Ladysmith during the South African War and fought in the 1906 Zulu Bambata Rebellion.

Officers of the 3rd SAI Battalion – Transvaal and Rhodesia.
Back Row: Capt Burrough, Lieut H M Hirzel, Capt R R Sharp, Lieut Wilson, Lieut A L Paxton, Lieut H G Elliot, Lieut A E Sharp.
Second Row: Lieut O H de B Thomas, Lieut J B Baker, Lieut D M Abel, Lieut Ellis, Lieut E J Phillips, Capt Perrol, Lieut Gardener, Sec-Lieut Bliss, Capt A W H MacDonald, Captain/ Dr S Liebson, Lieut H N Healey.
Seated: Capt D R McLachlan, Capt Sprenger, Capt Mills, Major Hemming, Major Young, Lieut-Col E F Thackeray (OC), Major Webber, Capt J W Jackson, Capt R F C Medlicott, Capt Montgomery, Capt E V Vivian.
Seated on ground: Lieut Rogers, Lieut Thompson, Lieut F W S Burton, Capt L W Tomlinson, Lieut B H L Dougherty. (Ditsong National Museum of Military History)

The 3rd Battalion (Transvaal and Rhodesia) was commanded by Lieut-Col Edward 'Frank' Thackeray, 45, the son of an Indian Mutiny Victoria Cross winner. He had been a cowboy in the USA, then in 1890 joined the British army and served in India. In 1896 he served in the Matabele Rebellion as a sergeant-major, then in the South African War as a trooper in the Relief of Mafeking and later as an officer in Kitchener's Fighting Scouts.

The 3rd Battalion's A Company was mainly from the Imperial Light Horse, B Company from Witwatersrand Rifles, C Company from the Rand Light Infantry and D Company from the rest of the Transvaal and Rhodesia.

Officers of the 4th SAI Battalion – SA Scottish.
Back Row: Sec-Lieut C S Bell, Lieut J Watkins, Lieut Micklem, Lieut J L Shenton, Lieut M L Norton, Lieut A Young VC, Capt F Mitchell, Lieut J French.
Middle Row: Lieut J McCubbin, Lieut R D Graham, Lieut H G Oughterson, Lieut R B Thorburn, Lieut C M Guest, Lieut A H Brown, Lieut C Duff, Sec-Lieut A Gemmell, Lieut T Farrell, Lieut A S Taylor, Lieut R D Grierson, Lieut W D Charlton, Lieut H M Newson, Lieut G Smith, Hon Lieut Z B Bayly, Lieut A M Cameron.
Front Row: Capt R Anderson, Capt E C Grady, Capt E G Clerk, Capt T H Ross, Capt S Thomson, Major D M Macleod DCM, Lieut-Col F A Jones DSO (OC), Capt C M Browne, Major/Dr M S Power, Major D R Hunt, Capt Morton, Capt G Mowat, Capt G E W Marshall.
Absent: Capt S C Russell, Capt H McVeigh, Sec-Lieut C Maclean.
(Ditsong National Museum of Military History)

The 4th Battalion (SA Scottish) was commanded by Lieut-Col Frank Jones DSO, 42, who had been awarded the DSO while serving with the Welsh Regiment at Paardeberg in the South African War.

The second in command, Major Donald MacLeod, 45, who had won the DCM at Omdurman, was in charge of A and D Companies, being the Cape Town Highlanders and various Natal and Caledonian Societies, while Major Donald Hunt, 41, commanded B and C Companies, from the 1st and 2nd Transvaal Scottish.

All the senior officers had served in the South West African campaign, as had most of the men. About 15% of the men were Afrikaners. This percentage would rise to 30% before the war's end.

From Cape Town the CPR (Cape Peninsula Rifles) was among the first units mobilised and was to form the core of the later Cape Town Company (1st Bn D Coy). One of its best sportsmen was Private Jack Carstens, 24, from Port Nolloth and later Wynberg Boys High School. He played cricket for Western Province and rugby for Villagers.

They formed a rugby team and decisively beat the local Potchefstroom clubs. Carstens played on the wing while his friend, Bill Carlson, played centre – as they had done at their 'Villagers' rugby club in Cape Town. When they went to celebrate they were inveigled into a game of 'Crown and Anchor' and ended up bankrupt – thereby forfeiting any chance of a party.

After kitting-out and initial training the brigade entrained for Cape Town and was then shipped to England. With them went two mascots: Jackie, a baboon belonging to Pte Albert Marr of the 3rd SAI, and Nancy, a springbok belonging to the SA Scottish.

The Voyage

The brigade left Cape Town on the *Dunvegan Castle* on 20 September 1915. According to Sec-Lieut Chauncey Reid the soldiers were soon prostrate:

> Seasick men all over the place; men too sick to move; the air could be cut with a knife; and the smell! As one of the men said to me, it was the nearest approach to Hell he had ever struck.

Private Jack Carstens had to endure it:

> We, the rank and file, lived in the ship's hold and slept in hammocks. The officers had their dining rooms, lounges and bunks. This was the one and only time that I regretted having refused a commission. But I and my friends had decided: no pips, no stripes; we are going to face this war as privates.

Fortunately things improved and by the time they reached Madeira on 6 October they had regained their sense of humour. Chauncey Reid recalled:

On the *Dunvegan Castle*. (J Carstens)

A crowd of small boats surrounded us as we anchored – boys diving for money, fruit hawkers and lace vendors and a miscellaneous assortment of humanity.

One police boat might have been out of Comic Cuts. Two marvellous looking sailors were pulling and two still more weird specimens stood in her stern. Dressed in dirty grey uniforms, armed with very long bayonets, swords and revolvers, their arms folded, they gazed about them with as dignified an air as it was possible for them to assume in a bobbing boat. They could not have looked more absurd.

The diving boys are beautifully developed. The row which arose from all the small boats was terrible … There has just been an alarm and I had to charge down to our troop deck. Nicholson, who shares my cabin, is so short that he can't reach the lifebelt rack, and I am afraid he will be drowned …

Friendships were kindled on board which only death would someday sever. Cyril 'Classy' Nicholson would be a fellow platoon leader in the Cape Town Company, as was William Nimmo Brown from Rondebosch, the son of a Cape Town magistrate.

On reaching Plymouth they disembarked in lighters, then entrained for Bordon, in Hampshire. Two officers per company and a proportion of the men were then given leave and Reid headed for London:

The night we arrived there was a Zeppelin raid and the windows on one side of our hotel were all smashed to smithereens. At the time we were in another hotel quite nearby. As soon as we heard the bombs bursting, we took the lift, climbed onto the roof and enjoyed a splendid view.

There was the Zepp, with all the searchlights converging on her and shells bursting all over the place, until she threw out a white sort of cloud, some kind of gas I suppose, and disappeared. When she had gone we went to look at the damage. Three bombs had been dropped round the same locality, two in the streets and one through a public house, where a number of men were killed. A bus had been badly shaken by one bomb and the conductor killed …

They toured London and also looked up friends:

Yesterday I went out with one of our officers named Style [Lieut Sydney Style from King William's Town] to see Mrs Dickis. It took us all the afternoon to get out there. We became so hopelessly lost in the Tubes. When we did eventually arrive, she was out!

Training in musketry and bayonet fighting followed:

The instructors are mostly men who have been in France, and they know what ought to be done.

It was bitterly cold during the training phase but they found time for leisure:

Style and I have been for any number of strolls round about the country, but, as it grows dark at 4.30 nowadays, we don't see much …

A representative from Elliott and Fry Ltd came down to our mess and took our photos, so that, if we happen to be killed, we will have the satisfaction of knowing that we will appear in the 'Sketch' and all the other papers in the Roll of Honour.

In the 2nd Battalion D Company Walter Giddy, 20, kept a detailed diary of events. He had been born at Barkley East in 1895 and attended Dale College in King William's Town. He had joined up with a number of friends; for example he was No 1613 while Sidney Phillips was No 1615.

On 12 November Giddy recalled the delights of discovering London:

Went for a weekend to London, 16 in a compartment. Arrived at Waterloo Station and hunted around, at last arrived at Waterloo Hotel, where we put up for the night after having supper.

Up early next morning, anxious to see as much of London as was possible in the short time at our disposal. We had breakfast at 7 o'clock. Had a look where the bombs were dropped by the Germans, then went to Crystal Palace, Westminster Abbey, Buckingham Palace, St Paul's Cathedral, Museum,

Madame Tussauds Waxworks, Chamber of Horrors, Houses of Parliament, Tower of London, and passed over the [Tower] bridge. Saw Mrs Pankhurst's residence, and old Bailey.

Sunday morning went to service at St Paul's Cathedral and watched the children feeding the pigeons on coming out. After lunch we went to Middlesex Street (Peddicoat Lane), then at last landed at Waterloo Station, with a bob [shilling] in my pocket and a return ticket to Bordon Camp.

Other Border recruits in the 2nd Bn D Company were George Garnet Tanner and his brothers Douglas and Stanley. On 10 September, 1914, as a member of the Kaffrarian Rifles en-route to the South West Africa Campaign, he was involved in the Hex River troop train disaster.

While descending the Hex River Pass control of the train was lost and the engine and eleven coaches derailed. Garnet Tanner realised that the train was derailing so leaped out through the window. The coach rolled and stopped an arm's length from crushing him.

He was hospitalised at Wynberg before proceeding for service to German South West Africa. After the campaign he was discharged suffering from poor eyesight. This did not preclude his being accepted for service with the brigade when it began recruiting at Potchefstroom.

Royal Approval

On 2 December 1915, Queen Mary inspected the battalion, as King George V's horse had fallen on him and he was incapacitated. The queen was accompanied by Prince Albert [later King George VI] and Princess Mary.

General Lukin called for cheers and Chauncey Reid recalled:

After three cheers, we gave her the South African war cry. She must have thought us mad …

The war cry went "Igamal'o Gahee! [three times, followed by:] "Wah!!!" The royal party in their car smiled, but Prince Albert laughed aloud. They then drove along the ranks inspecting the brigade and were duly impressed. Reid needn't have been concerned at how the march past would proceed.

Just before marching past, Captain Heal told the men in our company to give the queen the glad eye, so that they would turn their eyes to the right.

Walter Giddy (2nd Bn D Coy) recalled:

We were kept at the slope for ages, tiring but enjoyable.

A week later the battalion received embarkation orders, which pleased Reid:

> Yesterday we were told officially that we are going to Egypt. This means that a great deal of our kit is useless, but at least we will be warm, thank heaven! All of us are pleased. We are not afraid of Germans, but dread the cold. It is rather funny, because I have always wanted to go to Egypt, Persia and round that way.

Egypt

On 30 December the 1st, 2nd and 3rd Battalions embarked on the *Saxonia* from Devonport, near Plymouth. According to Walter Giddy (2nd Bn D Coy) on the 28th:

> Left Bordon at 11 o'clock at night and entrained at ten past one on the morning of the 29th. Were given sandwiches by the mayoress of Exeter. Afternoon on board the *Saxonia*. Trainload after trainload being brought in and marched straight on to the boat.

Maurice Woolf (1st Bn C Coy) was aboard. His father, Peter, from Kiev in the Ukraine had served in the Lichtenburg Commando during the South African War, while his mother, formerly Martha Coetzee, was a second cousin of President M T Steyn of the OFS. She and Maurice, then eight years old, spent much of the war in a concentration camp. He later attended the Christian Brother College in Kimberley, then served in German South West Africa.

The 4th Bn SA Scottish sailed on the SS *Oriana* on 2 January 1916, from Devonport. After eating rabbit cooked in new boilers, which had verdigris, the men suffered from ptomaine poisoning. There were insufficient lavatories for the 2,500 men and the deck of the ship became indescribable.

The Senussi Arabs under Gaafer Pasha were in revolt and Major-General Wallace of the Western Egyptian Force opposed them. The South African brigade initially encamped at Mex Camp near Alexandria.

The men from the *Saxonia* landed at Alexandria on the 11th and did a route march through the town. Giddy thought it one of the dirtiest places he had ever set eyes on. On the 16th he wrote:

> The chaps have been grousing all day long (The Australians call us 'Smuts bob-a-day tourists). Well this is a good name for us, as we don't seem to have the slightest chance of seeing any fighting, and we are going to do garrison work.

On the 21st they embarked for Mersa Matruh:

> Got off at 5.00pm. On trawlers, about 100 in each, and had an awful journey, everyone so ill. After 19 hours of misery, we at last landed. All my kit was drenched, as the sea washed right over the decks.

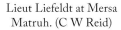

Lieut Liefeldt at Mersa Matruh. (C W Reid)

22nd. We landed at Matruh, and sand, nothing but sand as far as the eye can reach, not a sign of vegetation in sight. After a swim in the sea we felt a bit better. Are off at 4.00pm on an expedition inland, carrying night equipment. Water is very scarce here, only allowed a bottle a day, so far and get tea for breakfast and supper while in camp.

The Battle of Halazin

The 2nd Battalion was used in an attack on the Senussi at Halazin (near Mersa Matruh) on 23 January 1916. The 15th Sikhs attacked with the 2nd SAI in support. According to Pte Philip Cockroft:

> The sound of the guns became louder and louder. How impatient we were! The one great fear from which we all suffered seemed to be that the artillery and cavalry would 'finish them off' before we got a chance.
>
> On, on we went, laughing, singing, joking, until a halt was called just behind the guns. We were content to sit and watch the guns as they barked in quick succession. We were soon on our way again, but before reaching and passing the guns we were under fire … For the first time in history a South African force was in action overseas; this knowledge and the zest for battle kept away fatigue and held our spirits at high water mark.

Walter Giddy experienced his baptism of fire when they attacked over open ground in the face of artillery and machine-gun fire:

> Left camp daylight and travelled about seven miles, where our big guns opened fire on the enemy (Arabs and Turks), and the fight commenced.
>
> The Sikhs and D Company were 1st Line (firing line): The fire from the enemy was pretty hot, but we advanced in short rushes, and drove them quickly back.
>
> The Arabs used leaden bullets (mostly) and they made rotten wounds, but we had some marvellous escapes. One hit a couple of inches alongside my head, shot some sand down my back, that made me duck.

Sikhs are very cool in action. I was on the extreme left flank, and was lying alongside the Sikhs, and they were chatting to me, most of the time in broken English, some spoke good English, but some found it hard to make me understand. Australians, Sikhs, New Zealanders, South Africans and Royal Irish all took part in the fight.

They had a big gun and machine-guns, which kept us low for a bit, but we eventually got them on the run, and then the Australians rushed up and burned their village, and finished things off.

We lost 15 killed and over 100 wounded (South Africans), the others lost a lot too, but we could not find out the exact enemy's losses, as they carried most along with them. The fight lasted just over six hours. On our way back we extended and collected the dead and wounded (what was left of them as the Red Cross men were busy all the time).

Private Percy Land, 18, (2nd Bn D Coy) from King William's Town advanced until he was hit in the right leg by a bullet and collapsed in the dust. He would spend three months recuperating before rejoining his company.

Walter Giddy also acted as a stretcher-bearer:

We camped for the night about three miles from the 'scene of action' and the next day we had to carry our wounded on stretchers, as far as the Wells: It had rained heavily during the night, and the other ambulances could not come further than the Wells.

We had an awful time of it, my shoulders ached from carrying the stretcher, but I was more sore about the poor wounded, what with slipping and jolting and the hot sun and scarcity of water, they must have suffered severely. We camped at the Wells, could not get any further, and started the tedious march back to camp the next morning.

Reached camp about 5 o'clock, and a sorry lot we looked. Heaps of fellows knocked up, and were footsore so were brought in on wagons. I felt gone in when we reached here, but after a night's rest, felt a bit better.

Philip Cockroft agreed:

In a blinding sandstorm, the 2nd SAI, limping or dragging one foot after another, dirty, unshaven, as brown as the desert, but still smiling, reached their camp, having in exactly 72 hours, marched 60 miles, fought in a six-hour action, and undergone an experience which would not be easily forgotten by those who survived in spite of the greater and more trying ordeals which lay before them in France.

Meanwhile the rest of the brigade were still in reserve. Some of the officers and men went sightseeing. Second-Lieutenant Chauncey Reid and Lieut Walter Henry followed a guide, who held a candle, through tunnels into the centre of a pyramid. According to Reid:

> He then blew out the candle, and asked us how much we were going to give him. Luckily, we had an electric torch, so we told him that, if he didn't show us the way out pretty quickly, we would kick him out.
>
> We rode camels back to the tram, and were almost wobbled to bits. That evening, while we were having dinner at the Continental Hotel, we received word that we were to return to camp immediately, as we were about to move … One of our regiments [2nd] did us a shot in the eye by getting into action before we did, but we are keeping a strict lookout to see that they don't do it again.

They then moved to Mersa Matruh. The 1st Battalion D Company were encamped alongside a beautiful large lagoon according to Sec-Lieut Reid:

> Liefeldt [Lieut Aubrey Liefeldt] and I are at present on outpost duty on the seashore, and far away from all brass hats. We do as we like and dress as we fancy. If we had a change of menu we would be in clover. We live in a sort of dugout, made of sandbags. We eat our bully beef on a bully beef box and are supremely happy …

Relaxing in the desert. (C W Reid)

The Battle of Agagia

Reid's peace was short-lived for on 22 February Brig-Gen Lukin led the column, consisting of the Nottinghamshire Battery RHA, 1st SAI, 3rd SAI, 1/6th Royal Scots, Dorset Yeomanry and a squadron of the Royal Bucks Hussars, on a forced march to Agagia. On the afternoon of the 25th they were shelled. Captain G J Miller (1st Bn B Coy) was impressed by their advance:

> It was a magnificent sight to see the force advancing over the country which was perfectly flat as far as the eye could reach. The infantry platoons looked like darkish cardboard squares equidistant and moving steadily forward with now and then a brief halt. The column now left the coast road and moved inland in an almost southerly direction. Gradually the ground changed in nature and became undulating with some stony kopjes.

According to Reid:

> As soon as the Arabs opened fire, our guns came into action, and what with the banging of exploding shells and the booming of the guns, there was a fine hulla-baloo going on. We lay under any cover we could get for about half an hour, and were then sent out into the open to prevent an attack …

The following morning after 9.00am they again went into action. Private Albert Marr of the 3rd SAI was shot in the right shoulder. His pet baboon, Jackie, was an inseparable friend, and was beside himself with grief. He attempted to comfort the prostrate Marr and licked his wound until the stretcher bearers arrived.

Sec-Lieut Reid continued:

> After half an hour's wait, we received the order to advance, and the line went forward as steadily as could be. The men were grand. We were under shrapnel fire all the time, with spurts of dust rising round us, but there was not much rifle fire.
>
> We had advanced about 1,000 yards when the fun began. The 3rd were held up by fire, and, when we caught them up, we ran into it, too. Liefeldt on our extreme right got it hottest and my platoon on the left of his ran him a good second. We faced not only rifle fire from the front, but a machine-gun on the right flank. Thank goodness they didn't have our range – the bullets were whizzing over our heads!

Private Albert Marr and Jackie. (Ditsong National Museum of Military History)

Liefeldt had flat ground in front of him and had to advance by short rushes. We had a small hill about 100 yards in front of us, and I rushed my platoon straight across and managed to get a bit of cover. About 30 men of the 3rd were stuck behind this hill and every time a man showed himself, ping-ping would come the rifle and machine-gun bullets.

I was held up for a couple of minutes, In the meantime, the left of our line had advanced. We had to get on without any further delay, so I took everyone along, my platoon and the men of the 3rd. Our advance on their flank evidently scared the Arabs and their fire had slackened considerably. We reached the ridge they had been holding, but found they had retired, in fact it looked as if a general retirement had begun …

Private Jack Carstens (1st Bn D Coy) recalled their first engagement and their first casualty:

As we advanced the enemy bullets pinged past our heads. It was our baptism of fire and it was impressive to find no signs of panic or wavering.

Suddenly there was a cry from Sergeant Horwood and he dropped like a stone. He had been shot in the throat.

'Give me a cigarette', he said. I lit one. He inhaled, gave a sigh and rolled over dead.

Jack Carstens. (J Carstens)

Still the bullets whistled past until the final charge of the Dorset Yeomanry and the battle was over.

Private Geoffrey Lawrence, 20, (1st Bn C Coy) had attended St Andrew's College in Grahamstown. He recalled the battle:

> Bullets of all kinds were flying thickly about us – it was fortunate the Senussi were very poor marksmen. They were firing with all kinds of rifles, modern as well as old blunderbuss types, using home-made bullets that went bumbling by and some that turned over and over, said by our old soldiers to be sawn off pot legs.
>
> We stopped on a bushy rise overlooking a valley below and as we moved down I said to the old soldier beside me, 'There seems to be a lot of singing canaries around here'. 'Canaries be blowed', he said, 'those are bullets'.
>
> Another rise and into another valley where it seemed impossible to cross alive for bullets were flicking and spurting up the sand like raindrops on water. Still no enemy could be seen to fire at. We went down and up the next rise and at last could see our enemy and open fire. I got off fifteen rounds rapid at white fleeing and dodging figures. We advanced no further. Here I drank my last drop of water.

Senussi Arabs under guard.
(C W Reid)

The 200 horsemen of the Dorset Yeomanry routed the retiring Arabs and captured Gaafer Pasha. It was to be one of the last cavalry charges in modern warfare. Private Frank Maskew, 23, from Cape Town was highly impressed by this cavalry charge.

The South Africans suffered one officer and 16 men killed. They were buried, then many were dug up by the Senussi to steal their uniforms. Father Eustace Hill, who had served as a chaplain during the South African War, the 1906 Zulu Rebellion and German South West Africa, attended to the reburials.

The campaign was brought to a close and the South African brigade was thanked, then shipped to France.

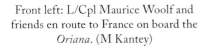
Front left: L/Cpl Maurice Woolf and friends en route to France on board the *Oriana*. (M Kantey)

The German Offensive.

The British Expeditionary Force and the invading German Army first clashed in France at Mons on Sunday, 23 August 1914. Within a week the victorious Gen Von Kluck's First Army had swept south through the Somme area. His IV Reserve Corps on the army's right flank had the distinction of overrunning the village of Longueval and the adjacent Delville Wood.

After passing the town of Albert, Von Kluck's army was ordered to swing south-eastwards. They were eventually stopped at the Battle of the Marne in early September 1914. A deadlock followed on the Western Front, to be relieved by the First Battle of Ypres in the north the following month. Both sides then dug in on a front-line stretching from Switzerland to the Channel.

The entire German military forces were headed by the Kaiser in his capacity as supreme war lord. Individual operations were led by the supreme army command under control of the chief of the general staff of the field army, Generaloberst Von Moltke. Due to ill-health he was succeeded on 14 September 1914, by Gen Erich Von Falkenhayn.

The Imperial Order

The German Empire, which was established in 1871, was a federation of kingdoms, principalities and of other noble rulers. As Prussia dominated the empire her king became the hereditary emperor.

The principalities had various degrees of autonomy, which their own armies and local governments, Saxony, Bavaria and Württenberg were called sovereign states, with much more autonomy than the other states.

The Bavarian army was not integrated with the Prussians as the other states tended to do, Bavaria still has a very free attitude today. The Bavarian Free State has its own border police and decorations and its own rather in dependent foreign policy which sometimes clashes with that of the Federal Government in Bonn.

Altenburg or Saxe-Altenburg and Prussian Saxony were of less importance. 'Prussian' Saxony was a part of Saxony lost to Prussia in 1816 as a penalty for Saxony having joined Napoleon on the losing side.

Thuringia (Thüringen) had been annexed to Saxony until 1815 when it fell under Prussia. The area was to be the scene of many prominent battles as it commanded the roads through central Germany.

The Imperial Army consisted of 24 Army Corps. Those not belonging to one of the sovereign states of Bavaria, Saxony and Württemberg were regarded as part of the Prussian Army. Only the Bavarian Army's Corps had their own numbers, I, II and III Corps.

Bavarian formations and units also had their own series of numbers. In terms of the law, contributions of manpower were in fixed proportions. Prussia and the small states provided 78%, Bavaria provided 11%, Saxony 7% and Württemberg 4%. Each of these four had their own war ministries, although the latter three only dealt with local arrangements.

The German War Effort

Germany was fighting on several fronts far removed from each other – Russia, Eastern Europe, Italy, etc. and on the Western Front: France and Belgium. Men and material were limited. The Allies had the rest of the world for support, whereas Germany had only its own resources. These resources had been heavily tapped and by mid-1916 were at their lowest ebb.

On the home front Germany was hard-pressed. Production of war material could not keep up with demand; raw materials were running out and manpower was at a premium. Men had to be replaced in farming, commerce and industry by women. Yet fortified by passionate patriotism and high ideals, the average German faced deprivation stoically, convinced of the righteousness of his cause.

Weapons

The German high explosive shells were given appropriate nicknames by the British; the sound of the Whizzbang (77 mm) came with the shell, giving no warning. The Jack Johnson or Coalbox (5.9 Howitzer-150 mm) gave off dirty black clouds of smoke. These shells bursting in soft ground would scoop a hole the size of a room. Lachrymatory (tear-gas) shells were fired and chlorine and mustard gas also used.

The troops used water-cooled Maxim Model 1908 machine-guns, stick grenades, the 7 mm Mauser and the 98 rifle with five-round magazines (7.92 mm) with Mauser action, 9 mm Luger parabellums, 52 cm or 37 cm bayonets and the new Flammenwerfer (flame throwers).

Steel helmets were only introduced in mid-1916. At first they were used only in isolated cases, and then only in the front lines. The withdrawing troops

Iron Cross and presentation case.
(P K A Digby)

would hand their helmets over to the men relieving them. Although initially regarded with disfavour, they were later universally introduced.

The Pickelhaube, reduced to its present size from the flamboyant parade helmets of the previous century because of practical considerations was still generally worn. Its bright trimmings were covered by a shaped canvas or felt cover in the uniform colour of field-grey, usually with the regimental number on the front. The Pickelhaube was a coveted souvenir for British troops, a fact the Germans were well aware of. In many instances retreating Germans had booby-trapped Pickelhauben in their recently vacated dugouts.

Formations

A German Army consisted of three corps. A corps in turn consisted of two to three divisions. A German Infantry Division (ID) had one or more brigades (IB), not to be confused with a British brigade. A German brigade usually consisted of two regiments. An Infantry Regiment (IR) had three battalions, each of which had some 750 to 800 men and formidable machine-gun fire. Thus the German regiment corresponded more closely to the British brigade.

A battalion consisted of four companies: Battalion I had Companies 1 to 4, Battalion II had Companies 5 to 8 and Battalion III had Companies 9 to 12.

The infantry strengths were:

	Officers	Other Ranks
Regimental staff	5	54
Regiment	83	3201
Battalion	25	1050
Company	5	259
Machine-Gun Coy	4	133

There were three machine-gun companies per regiment.

Strategic Considerations

General Von Falkenhayn wrote that the problem of the German High Command was basically a lack of manpower.

In March 1916 the German troops in Russia suffered serious losses in a surprise assault. An Austro-Hungarian attack in Tyrol was a disaster, and in March, too, the Germans suffered a further disastrous defeat in Lithuania with heavy losses.

The Germans were fighting on several fronts, with especially heavy losses in Russia, Rumania, Lithuania, Armenia, Iraq, Macedonia, Italy and on the Austria-Hungarian borders. It thus became imperative to send troops from the Western Front to support the sadly depleted forces on the various Eastern Fronts.

The troops left at Verdun were under heavy pressure and there appeared to be no visible proof of their success. At the same time intelligence reported massive mobilization of troops in England and in May reported that the enemy were forming up in large sections on the Somme.

2

French entrée

The brigade had a wonderful first impression of France, According to Sec-Lieut Chauncey Reid:

> We ran into Marseille. Really, I didn't think there could be such a variety of beautiful and interesting sights. We no sooner cease to wonder at one than we come across another. Marseilles is glorious from the sea side. I cannot describe it. You have seen pictures of towns on the Mediterranean, so that you will have an idea of what it is like.

Walter Giddy agreed:

> 20th [April 1916]. Reached Marseilles, a very pretty place, all wooded round the bay. Reminds me a lot of old England from the sea. The French soldiers at the harbour have very flashy uniforms, and their rifles with bayonet fixed, is longer than ours.
>
> A large passenger boat has just come in, her decks lined with (cheering) passengers. Two boatloads of Russians came in while we were in the harbour. They came right from Moscow round by Japan. We landed at 4.00pm and never entrained until 9.00pm but there was heaps to interest us – German prisoners, the French people, soldiers, etc.

The 4th SAI were quarantined for two weeks due to a case of spinal meningitis. One of the Transvaal Scottish, Private Arthur Betteridge 19, (4th Bn C Coy) had been born in Birmingham and became a railway telegraphist in Bloemhof. He joined the SA Scottish and after reaching Marseilles he recalled:

> As we marched out of the docks and through the streets of this lovely French seaport, women and children threw flowers and cheered the first kilted allied troops they had seen. The two weeks quarantine was a dreary business because we were forbidden to leave camp, and no one was allowed to visit us.

The SA Scottish arrive at Marseilles. (Transvaal Scottish Regimental Museum)

Some of the other battalion officers motored around the town and were struck by the pretty girls. Unfortunately they soon entrained, with Major Heal in command. Second-Lieutenant Reid (1st Bn D Coy) recalled:

> We had half a train load of New Zealanders with us. The train was stopped during meals and tea was supplied to the men at the stations. It was a great game. The train would run into a siding and out we would tumble for grub and to interview the inhabitants. Very funny interviews they were too.
>
> Nimmo Brown [from Rondebosch] is our linguist. At one station, Lyons I think it was – a very pretty girl and her family came down to have a look at us and offered Nimmo a franc or something for a badge. He didn't have one to spare, but collared a man who was passing and gave her his badge. Nimmo told her he didn't want the money, and that a kiss would suffice as payment. She kissed the <u>man</u> [the soldier instead of Nimmo]!

The trip might well have been fatal to Reid:

> At one station Major Heal and I were almost left behind. I was orderly officer and had to see all men into the train after a stop. The major was down with me when the train suddenly went off and we had to hang on as best we could. It wasn't bad until we passed through a tunnel and alongside a goods train. I was quite convinced that one of us would have his brains knocked out, but I was wrong …

The South Africans were to come up against the formidable German war machine at last.

Flanders

The train trip was enjoyed by all as they puffed through the beautiful French country-side. Walter Giddy wrote:

> Travelling north the country is very pretty. We pass fields upon fields of vines. They seem to go largely in for fruit growing … Very interested in the large vine field, River Seine, huge bridges across same, Hazebrouck, etc.
>
> 23rd. Disembarked and heard shells and were surprised to see our anti-aircraft guns shelling a German craft, and two of our aeros after her too.
>
> 25th First batch of SA [South Africans] off to the trenches. Issued us with two gas helmets and one steel one.
>
> 28th. Our chaps returned from the trenches and giving us glowing accounts of dangers and fun in them. We're attached to the 9th Division (Royal Scots, Camerons, Black Watch, HCJ).

The South African brigade arrived at La Bassee and was attached to the 9th (Scottish) Division, in place of the 28th Brigade, which had been decimated at Loos in September 1915. Initially resented, the colonials were soon accepted as their bearing, discipline and efficiency became apparent.

Some contend that it was because some Afrikaners couldn't speak English and could outshoot everyone, so were regarded as 'ware (true) Skotsmen'. . On their arrival in the line, a notice appeared above the German front line trench, welcoming the South Africans with the words, *'Welkom Afrikan Skotch'* – proof of the efficiency of German intelligence!

Gordon Smith (1st Bn B Coy) proudly wrote home:

> Very likely you have read in the papers that we are in the 9th Division. Of course you know what that means. We are the crack division of the whole Brit Army & that's saying something.
>
> We don't carry what other regiments do. We are not allowed to carry ½ an oz [ounce] more than is absolutely necessary for fighting purposes. Only personal equipment allowed is razor, shaving soap & brush, washing soap & towel. No corresponding of any sort to be carried. So you see we are not allowed to carry a writing pad. I always carry a few sheets of paper in my pay book.

The static conditions of trench warfare were initially difficult for the Springboks to adapt to, as they were used to free-ranging mobile warfare. The massive bombardments, constant machine-gunning and accurate sniping soon taught them to keep their heads down.

They were initially billeted at Le Bizet, close to where Lieut-Col Winston Churchill commanded the 6th Battalion of the Royal Scots Fusiliers. He had recently been dismissed from the Admiralty following the debacle at Gallipoli.

Private Harold Gwyn Ashworth 19, (1st Bn C Coy) had been raised in an intensely musical family. His father had immigrated in 1902 to become music master at Kimberley Boys High School. He had enlisted after the outbreak of war, aged 17, in a student force. According to him they were:

> ... clapped into the Castle in the centre of Cape Town and spent their first month of the war drilling by day, and my night chasing bugs with lighted candles and keeping watch on the ramparts for enemy aeroplanes. This is fact, not fiction.

He returned to his studies, but re-enlisted in August 1915, in the 1st SA Overseas Expeditionary Force. He served in 11 Platoon, C Company in England and Egypt with the brigade before arriving in France.

Ashworth said that there were four stages one went through as a combatant. To begin with there was simple terror where somehow discipline conquered your feelings and you did what was required. This was followed by a sense of bravado, a smile and a shrug when you escaped unhurt as a shell landed near you. The third stage was heralded by a sense of inevitability, your days were numbered in any event, it was pointless even caring. The final reaction was what we would now call 'post stress syndrome' but then 'shell shock'.

Private Cyril Weldon, 31, (1st Bn D Coy) was considerably older than most of his comrades. A former assistant private secretary to the Administrator of the Cape, he resented the fact that he had been overlooked for a commission.

On 21 April he wrote to his friend Vincent O'Reilly:

Cyril Weldon. (D O'Reilly)

Dear Vincent, Hope you are well and enjoying your visit to England. Have you got your commission yet? I gather from Aunt Margaret that there is some delay in the matter. My own application by the way is up the spout, owing, so I am told, to my being over 30 and this is held to be too old ...

Gordon Smith wrote home about their new situation:

I spent my Easter rather quietly. I was sleeping nearly all day under the trees in the country. We had been marching nearly all the previous night. I also went to Easter Holy Com{munion]. The Com was held where you don't often hear of Com being held in. For a church we had a timber shed nearly all the walls and roof blown away by enemy shell fire. The altar was a carpenter's bench & the seats were a couple of deals resting on cement casks. Now and again we couldn't hear what the parson was saying so loud was the roar of big guns & there was an incessant whine of the shells passing overhead. How's that for a novel place to hold Holy Communion in.

Talk about seeing things in England as regards aeroplanes. That's nothing to this. Over here we have aerial bombardments for breakfast dinner & tea. It is almost exciting to watch our planes going over the German lines & see the enormous amount of shells wasted in trying to bring our man down. It's no go though; they can't frighten him or any of them for that matter.

One day last week they must have used close on three hundred shells on one of our planes & he came back safe after all. The only part we don't like about the German shelling our planes is that the shrapnel bullets & pieces of shell come falling about our ears for usually our planes are almost above us when being fired on.

We haven't very much to fear though as the bullets invariably fall straight down & as we always wear our steel shrapnel helmets the pieces can't harm us unless they happen to be very large. A very noticeable thing about the farmers here is that they go about their farming as unconcernedly as if there wasn't such a thing as a war on & not so many miles from the firing line either.

Quite near enough for the stray bullets & shells to blot them out if they were unlucky enough to be in the way. They are even living in the same houses although they are half in ruins & they never know when another shell will come hurtling through the roof. Wherever one goes here one can see civilians & soldiers alike, men, women and children, all wearing satchels containing a gas helmet.

On 12 May Chauncey Reid was promoted lieutenant:

Most of the men are on fatigue, repairing trenches, cleaning drains and a hundred and one other jobs, all of them almost as safe as they would be on Cartwright's Corner [Cape Town]. If a man is fool enough to stick his head above the parapet, he gets a bullet. The Hun snipers are excellent shots. So are ours …

At night things are different. No sooner is it dark than star shells whiz up, like fireworks, all along the front.

Lieut Chauncey Reid. (C W Reid)

Machine-guns begin to rattle. Our sentries, by way of impressing upon the Germans that they are being watched, blaze off a round occasionally: not necessarily aiming at anything, but just trusting to luck. This goes on from stand-to in the evening until stand-to at dawn …

Wiring and patrolling are the most exciting jobs on earth. Over the parapet you go with a party, to repair the wire. Up goes a star shell, and you stand still as death for what seems an hour, till the light dies down. Then flat onto your stomachs as the machine-guns spit little devils at the spot where you were before. Very likely you haven't been seen, but you always imagine you have. Next, get on with wiring until the next star shell – and then the same performance again …

Our present abode is a house, the owner of which is goodness knows where. Thank heaven that he left his furniture behind! Nimmo [Brown] has been through a course on trench mortars. Nicholson is signalling officer. I have done a course of trench warfare. By the time the war ends, we will be jacks-of-all-trades.

Nimmo, as usual, is falling in love every few days. Someone has just suggested that Cupid has trained a maxim on him. Poor old Nimmo.

On 20 May Private Weldon (1st Bn D Coy) wrote to O'Reilly again about his commission and conditions:

… now that my own application seems to have fallen through, I do not feel inclined to press the matter. For one thing, I am quite content to remain with the contingent for they are a jolly good crowd and seem to have won the good opinion of the authorities … I am feeling quite fit still and so far have successfully dodged all the lethal devices invented by the Huns for one's undoing …

This morning, for instance, the enemy rudely interrupted my matutinal [morning occurrence] shave by chipping in with a series of high velocity shells, popularly known as 'whizz-bangs' …

It is quite a common occurrence for us to have a firework display of that kind; in fact, when I first came in there were two performances daily, though latterly we have been left alone. Shell fire is not nice, but for the absolute limit commend me to the poison gas act.

This ruddy invention is supposed to be very dangerous, in fact it is dangerous. One whiff of the horrid compound means, I am told, a painful, slow and lingering death …

The great thing is not to get wound up or excited, otherwise one is apt to do some fool thing such as shoving on the respirator back to front and so forth … Have not seen a German yet, except a few gangs of prisoners at various points on the train journey …

By the by, old man, if anything should happen to me out here I have asked my uncle to drop you a line and let you know about it … At present, it seems to me that it would merely be an unlucky fluke if one got hit, but one never knows when a big scrap might come … Your old pal, Cyril.

Lance-Corporal Maurice Woolf had been transferred to the Light Trench Mortar Battery on arriving in France. He recalled that one of their 'simpler' friends had been accosted by General Lukin, who said, "What are you doing, my man?":

> The man replied, "Sitting in the sun".
> The general retorted, "I can see that."
> The response was, "I'm warming my feet because I've got trench feet."
> Apparently the general responded, "If you don't get off that box, you'll get trench arse" …

The Somme

On 31 May the 9th Division marched southwards for 72 kilometres, to take part in the 'Big Push' close to the Somme River.

Chauncey Reid was to precede the 1st Battalion:

> Coming down, we marched, of course, and then I struck a fine job. At least, I thought it was going to be a fine job, billeting officer. With five NCO's and an interpreter, all of us mounted on bicycles except the interpreter, who had a horse, I went along 24 hours before the battalion, arranging billets …
>
> This billeting job is not so soft a thing as I thought. While the rest of the battalion are sitting tight and resting, we are working away ahead … It doesn't matter what happens, the billeting officer is expected to have billets ready, and he is strafed if he hasn't.

The March of the SAI Brigade

On 28 May Lance-Corporal Walter Giddy (2nd Bn D Coy) wrote:

> Off again to Bailleul for the night and on from there. I have to stay behind and act as guide to the incoming troops. Met the Durhams and guided them into Le Bizet, had supper at a café, and then stepped it out to Bailleul, where I found the boys billeted in a brewery. It must have been a fine place before the war, beautifully built machinery, just as the workmen had left it.
>
> 29th May 1916. Left Bailleul at 4 o'clock and arrived at a farm house where we were billeted in a stable. Immediately made love to the lady of the house, and got some fresh eggs and bread, and with this a tin of salmon that Sammy had brought along, we had a good supper …
>
> June 3rd 1916. Left Strazeele in the afternoon and passed through Hazebrook, quite a big place. We had an enjoyable march, but the kit was very heavy. Marching in heavy marching order. We were billeted in another farm house so Sammy and I had some more eggs and fresh bread and butter for supper. We also passed through Morbeque.

Walter Giddy. (J Morris)

4th. Marched on to a small village and were billeted in another barn. The march was hard, about 12 or 14 miles with full pack, we were all jolly tired and footsore, some dropped out. Sammy Heefe and I had our names taken (we were playing bridge and smoking in the barn) by Capt Hoppe [Hopcroft]

14th. On the move again, ordered to pack up. Marched 10 to 12 miles to Lillers, where we entrained and were put into the filthiest cattle trucks I have ever seen. We could not possibly sit down, so went back onto the stations and pinched a board which we sat upon.

15th. Passed through Amiens-de-Naimed and marched right

'Bonne chance mon camerade'. (*The War Illustrated* Vol IV)

through Amiens. It is an awfully pretty city, lovely parks, buildings, etc. Eventually landed at our digs (up in a loft), but awfully decent people. Sammy and I, as usual, went out to look for supper and landed in a café where we had a delicious meal, ending up with cherries, which weren't enough for two hungry Tommies, so we hunted in all the shops for more, but failed to find any, and seeing the trees were loaded, we entered the garden and consulted the old gardener as to the price of cherries. He gave us some but would not sell any.

We are billeted in a small village, Ally-Sur-Somme, just out of Amiens.

18th. Received M [Marching] Orders, 2.00am and were up at three, packed, entrained about six and arrived at our destination 10 o'clock. Sitting having our breakfast, first halt, have a nine mile march. Arrived here (Bray-Sur-Somme) in the afternoon after a stiff march and were billeted in canvas and wooden shacks. Had a wash in a canal of the Somme and supper, and are off again, order on work (trenches).

There is splendid fishing in the canals (Rouche and Perch). The French are on the other side of the canal. One can hardly describe the scenery about here, it is so pretty. There is a cornfield on our right, and the corn is intermixed with cornflowers and poppies, and the Somme on our left lined with trees and reeds.

All the tents and shacks are painted, so as not to be seen by the enemy aircraft, yet with all the peace and beauty I can hear the booming of the guns and occasionally the rattle of the maxims. Some French soldiers are fishing and seem to be having great sport. The sun is just setting and it is 9.00pm. It seems ridiculous.

19th. Back at 7.00am and off again at 11.00am and back at 9.00pm, tired out, in fact 14 [men] could not get here, and Capt Hophoff [Hoptroff] had four put in the guard room for falling out without permission (G Alger, K Roberts among the four).

Lieut Crede [Creed, 2nd Bn B Coy] (one of the CO [company] officers) did play the game with us. Even gave some fellows that were done up his tea and sandwiches. In a square mile behind our trenches they have 2,000 guns. We were brought through them on our way back. It was interesting.

20th. When going up to the trenches a mule wagon was standing on our left. The leaders were mounted but the rear drivers were round the wagon. A shell burst just over the wagon and off went the mules at a gallop, and they galloped about 400 yards before the poor chap on the leader could stop them.

21st. All went well and we were given an hour off, so Sid and I went off to the dry canteen. On our way up we were shelled. Sid dived into the long grass and I made myself as small as possible against a wall, and the shells just rained down. I got brick all over me. It got hot so we rushed for the nearest trench and made our way back.

Three Kings [men] were killed and 11 wounded. We got back 2 o'clock this morning. 6 o'clock we were off again. I was dead tired but we got back and had a bathe in the Somme. Another of 'The Kings' was killed by shrapnel while we were up in the trenches. The SA's have had luck so far.

The French say we are cold and reserved, we don't come and visit them. They are just across the river. Had a good look at the wonderful 75 [mm French Creusot gun]. Our particular camp is called Etineham.

22nd. Captain gave me a day off on account of feet being blistered.

The South African brigade had arrived near Corbie, on the Somme River between Amiens and Albert. According to Lieut Reid:

This portion of France is much prettier than the place we were in at first. Belgium and Northern France are awfully flat and very sparsely wooded. Here it is quite different. The country is hilly and there are any number of small forests, one of which we are at present occupying.

A river runs just below us, following a glorious valley. There is a canal too, which meanders along beside the river and has a path and trees fringing each side. Little tugs puff up and down, towing hospital barges, barges filled with RE [Royal Engineer] stores, ammunition and all kinds of things.

The men were employed mainly as working parties, carrying shells, ammunition and rations to the artillery positions around Maricourt, Carnoy and Suzanne.

Lieutenant Fred English, 23, was the second son of the magistrate and civil commissioner of Robertson, Western Cape. On 23 June he wrote to his sister from Corbie.

My dearest Maud,

Am still going strong along with the British army. Have seen a good deal of it too during the past week. Nothing but khakis wherever you go. We don't

Lieut Fred English. (Robertson Museum)

go from here for the simple reason that there's nowhere to go. We're on at endless fatigues at present, loading and unloading war material and do it with a certain amount of cheerful grinning.

Thank (heavens) our mess members all have a keen sense of humour, so that one can't do anything desperate. Great discussions are started and a good deal of leg-pulling. Our skipper (married) [Captain George Miller] is awfully jolly and clever …

I miss the shells and bangs in this place. All we hear is a dull Krump-Krump of heavy guns pretty far away. Aeroplanes are like 'aasvogels' … Haven't seen any hostile ones as we used to at Armentières … [On the 25th he continued] "This is to be a great event in my life, namely that we go into action soon and something big, very likely the biggest in these parts. None of us know who's to get through but all hope they're the lucky ones.

Should I get knocked out please don't feel rotten about it, but remember that I'm not the only one – merely a very small unit amongst millions. The whole sky was lit up last night by incessant gun flashes. This means the straff [strafe] has commenced. Very best of love and good luck to you all,
from Fred.

Lance-Corporal Walter Giddy (2nd Bn D Coy) continued:

23rd. 25 men were picked out and sent up to help the artillery. I happened to be one of them. We were brought part of the way on the G S wagon. It's a fine sight watching our artillery at work. The Huns have not retaliated as yet.

25th. Still pelting away at them, cutting their wire, etc. Sixteen French guns opened fire last night. It was one of the prettiest sights I have seen for a long time. It's wonderful the rapidity with which they fire. There was some mistake about our rations, and we have been lively on the R Fit since we left Etineham. Just about sick of it, as it was our officer's fault. One of our aeros dropped a bomb on our observation balloon. There was a flare and all 'Napoo'.

26th. Recalled to our regiment. Last night I took a message up to the Maricourt Wood to warn B Company. Left at 8 and got back at 10 o'clock, and a job it was too in the dark, tripping into shell holes. Our batteries were firing for all they were worth, they are still at it this morning. The Hun trenches must be in an awful state, and strange to say they have not retaliated.

We have 13 Observation balloons up this morning. We have to be careful (as we're between two batteries) of premature shells. Of a night our artillery fire looks grand for all bar the Huns. I was watching them for a long time bursting over the Huns firing line. It must have been hell for the poor wretches.

Reached a wood about six or seven miles back, where we reached the regiment. First thing I was after was post and was not disappointed either.

27th. We handed in our soft caps this morning and only have our steel helmets. A draft arrived from Bordon for us. Most of them were those knocked out of time in Egypt. I was quite sorry to leave the artillery. They were so nice to us.

Two platoons (15-16) left, but we were lucky enough to stay behind, as it is raining. The guns have been going all night and most of the day, hard. Saw Charles, Jimmy Cragg and Jess Cliverley for the first time since I landed in France.

29th. Had an instruction on the Lower Machine-Gun [Lewis-Gun?]. It's very simple to use and beautifully manufactured. The bombardment has slackened somewhat.

30th. Had another machine-gun instruction and just as it turned dark we packed up and made back to Bray. At first we could see the flash of the big guns and a faint boom, but as we approached it grew louder and louder. On the slopes of hills above Bray we were finally halted and turned in for the night.

The Germans at the Somme

Five divisions were withdrawn from the Western Front and sent to the Eastern Front. The remainder had to be spread out along the Western Front. At the start of the Somme Battle, the Germans had five divisions north of the Somme and three on the south. But as the battle increased in intensity and it became clear that this would be a massive invasion on a relatively small front, more troops were brought in from Verdun and from reserve positions. In mid-July the number of men on the Somme front had increased to such a degree that they could not be controlled from one point anymore.

The 1st Army under General dI Fritz von Below and his chief of staff, Oberst von Lossberg, was concentrated on the northern side of the Somme.

The southern sector was allocated to the 2nd Army under General dA Max von Gallwitz, who had just been brought to the Somme from the Maas and Verdun battle-field, and his general chief of staff, Oberst Bronsart von Schellendorff. Von Gallwitz was also given overall command over both army sectors.

The Supreme Command's original plan had been to launch a massive counter-attack against the enemy on the Somme and to stop the enemy's advance with one short sharp blow. However, the reverses suffered on the Eastern Front and the resultant necessity of depleting the troops on the Western Front brought this plan to nothing. The comparatively weak troops left to guard the Western Front were in no state to launch a massive counter-attack.

The Germans would be forced to defend their position with unbelievable tenacity in the face of overwhelming odds. Although there was an enormous disproportion between German and enemy troops, the enemy would not succeed in breaking through the German lines on the Somme. Enemy losses were extremely high. The Germans would hold onto every inch of territory with grim determination.

The Germans generally held the dominating positions, which they proceeded to fortify. Their lookout posts had fine views over France. In the Somme their commanding heights included the strong Thiepval ridge, the Bazentin ridges and the Longueval village ridge.

Certainly the greatest advantage the Germans possessed on the Somme was their prepared defences. In the nearly two years that they had occupied the area, they had excavated dugouts, some nearly forty feet deep. Churchill was to describe the Somme as 'undoubtedly the strongest and most perfectly defended position in the world'.

The first line in the Delville Wood area lay approximately 1.5 kilometres south of Montauban. It was the original front line occupied by both sides. The second line, the Braune Stellung trenches (Brown Line), ran just in front of the Bazentine ridges, Longueval and Delville Wood.

The village square – facing west. (T Fairgrieves)

From these heights Germans could see several miles beyond the old British front line. From the junction of Longueval and Delville Wood it ran south past Waterlot Farm (Sugar Factory) and a bombed-out house to the Guillemont Railway Station, then southwards to Falfemont Farm and Maurepas and the sunken road between Ginchy and Morval.

The Longueval village market place was at the crossroads. One road led northwards to Flers, another westward to Bazentin le Grand and Pozières, one southward to Montauban, one south-eastwards to Guillemont and another eastwards to Ginchy.

Immediately north-east of the village, adjoining and almost overshadowing it was Delville Wood, a thick tangle of oak and birch trees with a dense hazel undergrowth. The name of the wood came from the French 'Bois de la ville' (Wood of the village).

The wood was roughly 1,200 by 800 yards in size and offered a covered approach into the village. It was therefore essential to occupy both the wood and village if the latter was to be properly defended.

The German third line lay in the dead ground on the reverse northern slope of the Bazentin-Longueval ridge. This was known by them as the Foureaux Riegel (Wedge) and by the Allies as 'The Switch Line'. Although only partially completed, it was to prove essential to the German defences of High Wood (Foureaux Wald) and Delville Wood.

As the German divisional headquarters was at the village of Flers, it was to be protected at all costs. The strategic village of Longueval to the south, although falling between the last two defensive lines, would have to be held to keep the enemy from assaulting Flers itself.

The Germans methodically tunnelled into the soft chalky ridges, sinking dugouts and preparing concrete bunkers and wired strong points. In the village of Longueval tunnels connected basements of houses to each other and to strongpoint's in the adjoining Delville Wood. The church and chateau in Longueval and Waterlot Farm were properly connected by tunnels with the wood.

Although defences in Delville Wood had been started, they had not been completed and due to some blunder from higher up, the wood was not defended when the July 1916 assault commenced. The Germans were so occupied with their front lines in Trônes and Mametz Woods, at the Sugar Factory and in Guillemont, that they had ignored the danger Delville Wood could prove to be.

3

The Big Push

For the last week of June the British artillery would bombard the German positions in order to 'soften them up' and destroy the barbed wire strung before their positions on the heights.

On 29 June Pte Cyril Weldon (1st Bn D Coy) again wrote to O'Reilly:

Wale, Williams, Allison, Holiday and other friends are all well and have asked to be remembered to you. They also desire me to send you their hearty congrats [on being commissioned in the Coldstream Guards]. I myself, I am pleased to say, continue in good health and am even alleged to waxing fat.

Don't know when I shall be able to get this letter away – if ever. We are on the move a good deal and judging from the racket of guns that goes on somewhere away in front I should say that the people there must be on heat. Haven't seen a paper for days, so don't know at all how the war is going, but everyone seems to be full of beans and optimism.

Shouldn't be surprised if we suddenly struck a big scrap one of these fine days … Wonder if by any chance we shall at any time run across one another out there. Goodbye old man and may the best of luck always attend you.

Your old pal,

Cyril."

On the night of 30 June the brigade moved to Grove Town Camp, where the division assembled. It would be in reserve for the attack on the German positions on a 14 mile front the following day.

Some men had a premonition of death. Second-Lieutenant Allan Haarhof (1st Bn C Coy) confided in his younger friend Pte Gwyn Ashworth. They had been close friends before joining up and Gwyn, the son of the music master at Kimberley Boys High, resented the fact that he had been overlooked when others were offered commissions.

Officers were expected to consort only with fellow officers and not with enlisted men. Ashworth wrote in a letter home that:

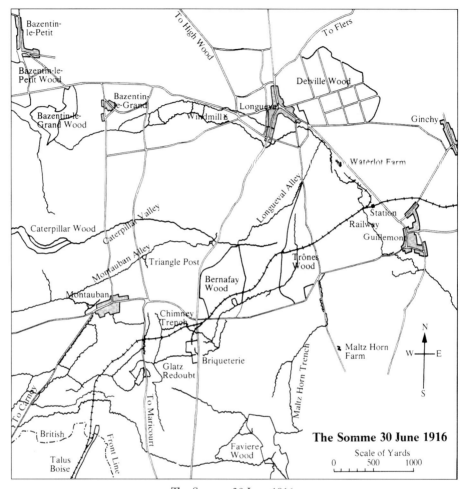

The Somme 30 June 1916.

Mrs Haarhof was quite right when she said that a 'star' would make no difference to Allan <u>but</u> at the same time there is a very definite line of demarcation between officers <u>and</u> men in the army. We have to meet in a clandestine fashion in the night and only when out of distance of prying eyes during the day.

On the day before the Somme battle commenced Haarhoff intimated to Ashworth that he did not think he would survive the coming conflagration. As a signaller attached to headquarters Ashworth stood a better chance of surviving than he, an officer who would lead his men in attacks over open ground.

Haarhof gave his silver pocket watch dated 1879, an early top winder, to Ashworth as a memento. The latter had always shown an element of hero worship toward him, as well as fraternal friendship.

1 July – The First Line

The long-awaited attack took place on 1 July, after a week's bombardment of the German lines. The troops were told to advance at a walking pace as the enemy's wire and trenches would be obliterated. At Contalmaison the East Surreys moved across No-Man's-Land while dribbling footballs.

In fact, for a week the guns had fired shrapnel shells, instead of high explosives, and the wire had not been damaged. The Germans emerged from their deep dugouts, manned their machine-guns and mowed down the attacking forces. That day the allies incurred over 60,000 casualties, of whom some 20,000 were killed.

The carnage wrought by the entrenched Germans on the over-confident Allies was due to their having weathered the week-long bombardment in the security of their dugouts. When the British attacked they never expected much opposition from the supposed shell-blasted enemy.

Nevertheless, in the Albert sector during the following few days the German first line fell and they lost the village of Montauban, which had been reduced to rubble by the British bombardment.

The attack. (*The War Illustrated* Vol V)

Lieutenant Chauncey Reid (1st Bn D Coy) was optimistic about the offensive:

Our division was in reserve, so we bivouacked behind the line among the guns and in the most infernal din I have ever heard. This shelling went on until the morning of the first, when suddenly the guns simply rolled!

Hundreds of shells were screeching over every minute. This lasted for about half an hour. Then it stopped and the infantry went over. We sat and waited, ready to leave at any moment, for about two hours. At last we got tidings from Divisional Headquarters that the German first line had been taken. Every hour or so messages arrived, to the effect that trenches had been captured.

We followed the whole advance on our maps. Everything went swimmingly and, towards afternoon, prisoners started coming in. A miserable, woebegone crowd they were. They had been unable to get rations up to their trenches for a week or so, and had suffered a shelling they had never dreamed of. They were all overjoyed at being captured.

We put them into barbed wire enclosures, which had been prepared before-hand. Our little interpreter was in great form, interpreting for the intelligence officers. Two of us went down to see what the Germans were like, and were gazing at them, when up minced our little interpreter – and asked us if we had seen the [German] colonel. We told him we hadn't and he said, 'Come along. Colonels are in the next cage!' It was for all the world as if we were inspecting animals at the zoo …

A few days later we set out to take over trenches from a brigade [at Briqueterie] that had been in them since the beginning. I had been up the day previous to see the way, so I had to lead the battalion up. There was so much traffic, ammunition wagons, ambulances, RE Stores and goodness knows what else that it took us three hours to cover the mile.

Eventually, about 1.00am, we arrived at the trenches and, as soon as the others were out, started work on parapets, traverses, etc. All that night we worked and all the next day, the next night and the next day, keeping it up until we were relieved five days later.

Nobody had had enough sleep. I had four hours, made up of half hours here and there. We were shelled every day and every night, till we were sick of the sound of the guns – ours and theirs. My platoon was holding a bit of trench [immediately south of Bernafay Wood], Nimmo [Brown] supporting with a trench mortar and Larmuth's platoon was just behind us …

Walter Giddy (2nd Bn D Coy) had a different perspective:

July 1st 1916. Roused at sunrise by the roar of artillery; they were going like machine-guns and have kept it up ever since. The divisions we were supporting have advanced right past the Hun lines and we have got to be ready to move at any moment (10 minutes notice).

The attack on Montauban. (*The War Illustrated* Vol V)

A mine was exploded, the smoke rose like a large thunder cloud. Batch after batch of Hun prisoners and wounded have been sent back through our lines to the rear. Willie de Wet has just driven our water-cart away for more water. He is an old Aliwal [North] boy. Everybody seems busy rushing about. I guess it's an anxious time for those responsible in a big advance like this.

An aero sailed down on fire; she was planing down at a duce of a rate and just dipped over the horizon. Up went a cloud of smoke. I don't know if pilot had time to jump out.

We had a general and other officers in the Prisoners' Camp. I'd never dream a big advance was taking place; our fellows are kicking a football about, others singing and various SA parties have gone out to consolidate the positions taken by the other divisions. Yet, on the other hand, the artillery is blazing away and a German observation balloon was bombed and all I saw was a pillar of smoke.

2nd. Left Bray and marched on to Suzanne Valley. Got to be more careful here. Sykes [Pte F Sykes] and I were having a wash-down when half a gas-lamp came hissing through the air and struck alongside him. It appears one of our guns bust, another small shell dropped among our fellows, but did not burst.

The valley is 'lousy' with French guns and they seem to shake the very earth. In taking the Hun trenches there were six men and a lieutenant left out of a platoon of the Surreys. They captured a lot of prisoners and did not know what to do with them, so they told them to run back to our lines, but they were all shot before they got there, bar one, who just laid down on top of the parapet.

They are keeping us in reserve in case the other divisions are driven back. A wounded man was coming back to the dressing station to have his arm dressed when he came across seven Germans. They immediately threw down their arms and he brought them in as prisoners. They said they were delighted to give themselves up. Five of their comrades who wanted to surrender were shot by their officer.

A party were watching a 6" Howitzer when the RFA [Royal Field Artillery] corporal asked Cpl Mallet if he would like to fire a shot. He did and he says he thought his head was splitting by the deafening roar.

1 July 1916. Still lying low in Suzanne Valley. The artillery are quietly moving up. We shifted up behind our old firing line, where the advance started two or three days ago. The dead are lying about. Germans and our men as well, haven't had time to bury them. The trenches were nailed to the ground, and dead-man's-land looked like a ploughed field, heaps must be buried underneath.

Montauban Wood was wrecked by shell fire, large trees cut and broken like matchwood; they tried to take Montauban Village at the point of the bayonet, but the loss of life being too great, the artillery was turned on it. The Germans came out and surrendered. They had had enough of it in the wood.

Rumour had it that the French cavalry is over and did successful work. While sitting here a Hun shell hit about 20 yards over us, but fortunately did not burst, the ground being too soft. Rained heavily today; everything is muddy, including myself.

5th July 1916. We were admiring the 7.15 [French 75mm cannon?] when the gunner let us have a shot or two out of it. They're very obliging, but I find it hard to make them understand.

It rained last night and we only have overcoats and waterproof sheets, but I cuddled up to old Fatty Roe, and slept quite warmly. There are no dug-outs where we are at present, and the shells are exploding uncomfortably near.

Had a man wounded last night for a kick-off. The Huns are lying in heaps, one I noticed in particular had both legs blown off, and his head bashed in. Some have turned quite black from exposure. They are burying them as fast as possible. Brought an old fashioned powder horn, Hun bullets, nose-caps of shells, etc, back with me, but I suppose they'll be thrown away.

6th. Told to hold ourselves in readiness, expecting an attack. Received draft (£5) from father."

Lieut Chauncey Reid (1st Bn D Coy) continued:

One morning [6 July] we watched the French attack Favier Wood. It was awfully interesting. The German trenches were at the bottom of a valley and we couldn't see them from where we were. They could only see us from Trônes Wood …

I was sent out with six men as soon as it was dark, to locate the German trenches and find out whether they were putting out wire, etc. When we left our trench, we were being shelled by the Germans, and when we got near the German lines we came under our own fire, so that we had quite a lively time.

After locating the trenches and ascertaining that no wire was being put out, we started back, had a breather between the lines when no shells were falling and arrived at our own trenches shortly after midnight. If the Germans had counter-attacked my patrol and I would have ceased to exist.

The first thing I heard when I returned was that Nimmo had been killed. He was just mounting his Stokes gun [at Chimney Trench] when a shell burst

Lieut W Nimmo Brown.
(*South Africa Magazine*)

right in the emplacement, killing one of his men as well. He was buried up to the armpits. One of my corporals was also buried, but not hurt. Poor old Nimmo. We buried him the following morning, with the man who was killed alongside him, and put up a cross to mark the place.

We didn't feel his death so much just then. There were so many ghastly things in and about that trench. Strewn over the ground immediately in front were about twenty dead Germans, the nearest lying on his back with his head over the parapet. We handed him over as trench stores to the people who relieved us. He was highly objectionable by that time …

Down to the right front there was a row of dugouts, beautifully made, with steps leading down, stoves for warmth, bookshelves, etc. These had been occupied by [German] officers. Five colonels, including the interpreter's, were captured here.

In front of these dugouts there were a few more Germans and, scattered all over the place, German equipment of every sort, rifles, bayonets, gas masks, cartridges, helmets, bombs – fine souvenirs any and all of them, but impossible to carry. We were not sorry to see the last of that locality. In my platoon there were eight casualties, including two killed.

Lieutenant Sandy Young (4th Bn D Coy) was to show why he wore the ribbon of the Victoria Cross. According to a special correspondent of Reuters Agency, while Young was engaged in repairing a signalling apparatus:

He saw lying under the enemy fire a French officer with a shattered leg. In spite of the terrific fire he picked up the officer and carried him out of the danger zone, whereupon the officer took the Legion of Honour from his tunic, and pinned it on his gallant rescuer …

Walter Giddy (2nd Bn) also had dealings with the French:

> 7th July: Made to sleep in the trench on account of the Hun shells flying a bit too near, had a cold rough night, but things have quietened a bit this morning, so we are back in our little shack made out of waterproofs.
>
> Bloody Fritz, he had started shelling the road, about 400 yards away and directly in line of us. A Frenchie was standing on the parapet and was excitedly beckoning to us. He'd put up his hands and point to a communication trench ahead. Couldn't make out what the beggar was driving at, so we ran up to him, and ahead were dozens of Hun prisoners filing out of the trench. It rained so hard our shack was just a mud-pool, busy drying our kit.

Bernafay Wood and Trônes Wood

On Saturday 8 July the 2nd SAI HQ, together with A and C Companies, relieved the 27th Brigade in Bernafay Wood. They were joined the following day by D Company. The 4th SAI A and C Companies advanced into Trônes Wood. The German shelling of the wood was heavy and many of the men suffered head injuries. The 2nd Battalion incurred over 200 casualties in two days.

Walter Giddy was among those under artillery fire:

> 8th. 3rd SA's were relieved by the Yorks who went over this morning 400 strong and returned 150 strong. Then our SA Scottish went over with a couple of the regiments and took the wood, and I believe lost heavily, but are still holding the wood. Seaforth, Black Watch, Cameron, PA, GPS are going over in the morning, so there will be some bloodshed, if they get at close quarters with cold steel.
>
> Hun sent over some Tear Shells, which made our eyes smart, but were too far to cause much trouble. Two of our companies were up to the firing line … I'd love to see the four 'Jock' Regiments go over in the morning. The Huns hate them like poison, yet I do not think their hate exceeds their fear.

Shellburst.
(Ditsong National Museum of Military History)

9 July. Shall never forget it, as long as I live. Coming up the trench we were shelled the whole time, and to see a string of wounded making their way to a dressing station, those who can walk or hobble along; another chap had half of his head taken off, and was sitting in a huddled up position, on the side of the trench, blood streaming on to his boots, and Jock lay not five yards further with his stomach all burst open, in the middle of the trench. Those are only a few instances of the gruesome sights we see daily.

As I am writing here, a big shell plonked into the soft earth, covering me with dust, one by one they are bursting around us. I am just wondering if the next will catch us (no it was just over). Oh! I thought one would get us, it plonked slick in our trench and killed old Fatty Roe, and wounded Keefe, Sammy who was next to me, and Sid Phillips [who joined up with him], poor beggar, he is still lying next to me, the stretcher bearers are too busy to fetch him away.

The Manchesters had to evacuate the wood below us, and we the one along here [Bernafay]. I'm wondering if we will be able to hold this wood, in case of an attack, as our number is so diminished. I've seen so cruel sights today. I was all covered in my little dug out, when old Sammy was wounded, [I] had a miraculous escape."

On 10 July Captain Russell (4th Bn A Coy) was mortally wounded in Trônes Wood. Meanwhile Private Walter Giddy continued describing the hell in Bernafay Wood:

10th. Still hanging on, and the shells flying round, three more of our fellows wounded, out of our platoon. Took Fatty Roe's valuables off him and handed them over to Sergeant Restall (he was an Imperial corporal in the Boer War and says he remembers when a span of oxen were commandeered from father).

We have no dug-outs, just an open trench. Of course, we've dug a bit, but it's no protection against those big German shells. Our chaps did so well at first. I thought we were going right through with it, as our cavalry was waiting in readiness, but I suppose we have got to expect these things.

Harold Alger has been badly knocked about. I'm afraid he won't pull through, arm and leg shattered by shrapnel. I had a lucky escape while talking to Lieutenant Davis, a piece of shrapnel hit on my steel helmet, and glanced past his head. He remarked 'That saved you from a nasty wound' (referring to the helmet). The SA lads in our platoon have stuck it splendidly, it has been a tough trial this.

We heard cries from the wood further down, and Geoghan and Edkins went to investigate, finding three wounded men lying down in the open. They had been lying there three days among their own dead, and had been buried a couple of times by their own shells, and the one brought in had been wounded again. They asked for four volunteers to bring in the other two, so off we went. It was an awful half hour, but we were well repaid by the grateful looks on their haggard faces. Poor old Geoghan was hit, his head was split off by shrapnel. Four of us buried him this morning.

German POW's assisting Tommy stretcher-bearers.
(Ditsong National Museum of Military History)

The SA Scottish HQ and B and D Companies then relieved the 2nd Battalion in Bernafay Wood. Giddy continued:

> 11th. We were relieved by our own Scottish, and are back at our former camping ground, but I do feel so lonely, out of our mess of five, only two of us left and my half section gone as well. We were right through the Egyptian Campaign too, as half sections.
>
> A Yorkshire man brought a prisoner over this morning, while we were still in the trenches, and he halted to have a chat. Our corporal could speak German, so he gave the prisoner a cig[arette] and he told us all we wanted to know. He was a Saxon and was heartily sick of the war, and our artillery was playing up havoc with their infantry, since the beginning of the Battle of the Somme. I didn't say anything, but their artillery had given our men as much as they could bear.

On 11 July at 6.45pm as Lieut-Col Jones exited his dugout a shell burst in the entrance, killing him. As it was a former enemy dugout the entrance then faced the German lines, with no defence against incoming shells. His death was a considerable shock to the men. Private Harry Cooper (3rd Bn C Coy) was a runner who saw Jones' body:

An ordinary soldier, yes, but not a colonel. I then began to realise that this was not going to be the fun we had expected. This was war!

Major Macleod DCM replaced Major Hunt on the 12th in Bernafay Wood and the latter returned to his company at Glatz Redoubt. That day the Germans concentrated their shelling on Bernafay Wood.

Private Giddy recalled the many deaths by shell fire.

12 July. About two miles back and still the Huns had the neck to put a shell into us. The Rev Cook was killed while helping to carry in wounded. I have just been watching the Huns shelling the wood we came out of yesterday [Bernafay]. It looks as though the wood is on fire, the smoke rising from the bursting shells. The Scottish (ours) relieved us too, and we lost 16 out of our platoon in it. It was a cruel three days, especially when Manchesters were driven out of the woods, 700 yards, in front of us, we were expecting the Huns over any minute, but the Huns would have got a warm reception. Then the Bedfords retook the wood, the full morning, which strengthened our position.

13 July. Allyman [Allemagne = Germans] found us again bending. I thought we were so safe for a bit. A shell plonked into the next dug-out to mine, killing Smithy and wounding Edkins, Lonsdale, Redwood and Bob Thompson, three of them belonging to our section. Only three of us left in Sammy's old section. It's a cruel war this. Just going up to dig graves to bury our dead. We buried Private Redwood, Smith and Colonel Jones, of the Scottish. General Lukin was at the funeral, he did look so worried and old.

On the 13th the 4th SAI were relieved by two battalions of the 55th Brigade (18th Division). The SAI Brigade then camped at Talus Bois, as the 9th Division's reserve brigade. Lieutenant Chauncey Reid (1st Bn D Coy) found that being in reserve didn't mean being out of danger.

I had a sentry group on a sunken road to the right of our position and one night a report came up that a German had been shot. On investigation he proved to be a Frenchman who was carrying bread to his section, but had lost himself. We ate the bread.

Coming out for a rest was a perfect nightmare. On some open ground we had to cross we found a French battalion going out to dig trenches, and six of them took cover in a shell hole and were blown to smithereens. The damage was done by a shell, which dropped in the middle of them. It didn't cheer the rest of them, or my men either.

The journey took us three hours, through all kinds of trenches, all alike in one respect – ankle-deep in mud. It had been raining for two days. That tramp just about finished us. Men loaded up with bombs, shovels, picks, camp kettles and ammunition, who have had scarcely any sleep for five days are not in the best condition for a tramp like that.

Liefeldt met us near the place to which we were bound – our old front line trenches – but, when we arrived, we found other troops in occupation. So we had to lie down and sleep where we were. As it was pouring with rain and we had a waterproof sheet each, you can imagine our dilemma. We didn't know whether to put the sheet underneath to keep us off the wet ground, or on top to keep the rain off.

We were so tired that we did sleep, but everyone was up at daybreak next morning and fires started to flicker all over the place. We were so cold and miserable that we didn't care if we were shelled. Men foregathered at the fires to dry and get a bit of warmth. They were a sight – officers just as bad as men. We were mud from head to foot, not just sploshes here and there, but one solid cake! Even our hair was matted together, and, as we hadn't shaved for at least a week, we were a queer-looking crowd.

We managed to get some rest that day, but the next morning were treated to some shell fire. It did not last long, however, and, having become more or less used to it, we treated it with disdain.

The next day a platoon which had been behind on dump work came up, and, as there was no room in the trench for them, started to make dugouts. The Germans spotted them from one of their balloons, and, imagining that they were building gun emplacements, opened fire. Of course, everyone took cover, and we only had two casualties in the company – but twelve rifles were smashed.

This sort of thing went on until the fourteenth, with working parties at night to add a little excitement. You can't imagine how quickly men can dig when they are being shelled. You can almost see them sinking into the ground!

German Reaction

Due to the heavy pressure on the German defences and the confusion resulting from fresh units arriving, the German structure had to be hastily reorganized.

The front was divided into corps sectors, within which the corps commander, his staff, heavy artillery and commissariat remained unaltered. The corps ceased to act as a fighting unit but rather as a framework within which the various divisions and brigades operated.

This solved the problem of command where such a multitude of units came and was to provide continuity of direction throughout a protracted battle. The Germans were to continue this system until the end of the war.

The front from the Somme to the Ancre was thus split into three sectors: Group Gossler from the Somme to Hardecourt, Group Sixt von Armin from Hardecourt to Pozières and Group Stein from Pozières across the Ancre to Gommecourt.

The British attack on the German second line would be launched against Sixt von Armin's centre group, where elements of the 10th Bavarian Division held the Braune

A shattered German trench and dugout. (Ditsong National Museum of Military History)

Stellung from Guillemont to Bazentin Le Grand and the 7th Division from there to Pozières. The 8th Division was in reserve south of Bapaume.

Most of the German heavy artillery on the Western front was massed at Verdun. When the Somme offensive was launched, the German army, though not quite taken by surprise, was none-the-less badly equipped to withstand the assault. Statistics show the overwhelming odds against the Germans: 70 German divisions were spread along the Western Front in the face of 105 British and French divisions.

The History of the Royal Prussian 4th Thüringian IR 72 aptly describes the Somme offensive from the German point of view:

> The great Somme battle had begun at the end of June 1916. On a broad front English and French troops were attempting to break through the German iron front, using massive amounts of troops and material, including strong air cover. The battle was opened on the 24th of June with a seven-day continuous heavy bombardment of incredible measure along the section Bapaume-Albert-Peronne.
>
> The enemy's greatest undertaking in the war so far was intended to break German resistance on a 40 kilometre front between the Ancre and the Somme. Cambrai-LeCateau-Maubeuge was the objectives of the far-reaching operation.
>
> At first the line Bapaume-Peronne was to be attained at all costs, from where it seemed easily feasible to turn the flank of the German front along the second line of defence. More than 30 French and English divisions were assembled along a fairly short stretch in order to gain the objective with the help of over-whelming odds.

If our adversary did not succeed in this aim, even by use of till then unheard of masses of men and ammunition, and if even the English themselves admitted to this fact later on, the part played by the German soldier cannot be sufficiently honoured.

The tenacity shown by the German troops, their endurance, courage and sense of duty in the face of overwhelming odds must be admired. And so under continuous bombardment and heavy losses the Germans managed to stem the tide of the enemy.

4

The Village – Friday 14 July (Bastille Day)

After suffering approximately 1,000 casualties in Bernafay and Trônes Woods the South African Brigade was reinforced by 500 men from their Bordon base. At midnight on the 13th July the brigade consisted of 121 officers and 3,032 men.

Longueval village is in the centre of a network of roads and is situated on an east-west ridge, which overlooks Montauban Village and Bernafay and Trônes Woods. The village of Flers is in the dead ground behind it. The adjacent Delville Wood is so-named as it is the *Bois de la ville* (Wood of the village).

The Longueval town hall and school – pre 1914. (T Fairgrieves)

The village was protected by lines of trenches and barbed wire, with numerous tunnels and inter-connecting strong points. The wood was bisected by roadways (rides) which were used for bringing out wood. The British gave names of London and Edinburgh streets to them to facilitate communication between units.

3.25am: The Scottish 26th and 27th Brigades of the 9th Division set off from the destroyed Montauban village and attacked Longueval village. The survivors of the German IR16 Regiment (Bavarians) held on to northern Longueval and stopped the Scots with raking machine-gun fire.

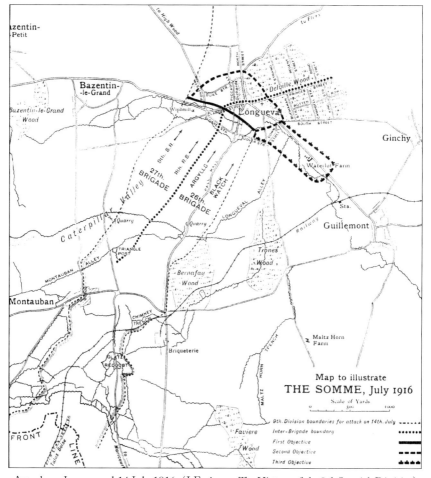

Attack on Longueval 14 July 1916. (J Ewing – *The History of the 9th Scottish Division*)

According to Major J Ewing in 'The History of the 9th Scottish Division':

The possession of the Longueval plateau was the key to the operations against High Wood in the north, and if the village was not taken, the plans of Sir Douglas Haig would be thrown out of gear. Moreover it was from Longueval that the attack on Delville Wood was to be launched; without it the operation would be more intricate …

It was clear that the northern part of Longueval could not be cleared by a casual or haphazard attack. The enclosed nature of the oblong of orchards made it difficult to locate the enemy's posts with certainty, and the artillery were handicapped by the want of a post, from which to observe the fire.

The problem was in fact more intricate than was realised at the time. The battering that the village had received from our guns had only been sufficient to convert it into a stronghold of immense strength.

Amidst the jagged and tumbled masonry the defenders had numerous well-protected corners from which they could fire without being detected, and the oblong was full of shelters where the garrison could take refuge from the fire of field guns.

The whole area needed to be pulverised by heavy shells, as General Furse realised [Furse's brother was a bishop in Johannesburg]. Against infantry alone the place was virtually impregnable, since the scope for manoeuvring was limited and all the approaches were swept by the fire of the defenders.

Major General Furse's request for a heavy bombardment was turned down by the Corps commander, Lieut General Sir Walter Congreve VC. The latter insisted that Longueval should be taken as soon as possible, which precluded the withdrawal of infantry and the preparation for a heavy artillery barrage. Furse therefore had to depend on his own limited artillery.

As regards logistics the Pioneer battalion of the 9th Division was the 9th Seaforth Highlanders. It was split up as follows: A Company to the 26th Brigade, B Company to the South African Brigade, C Company to the 27th Brigade and D Company remained in the rear repairing and building roads and tramways.

On 14 July A Company proceeded to Longueval to construct strong points and communication trenches. Due to enemy shelling B Company dug trenches until 11.00pm that night.

Walter Giddy (2nd Bn D Coy) was beginning to fret at their inactivity:

14th. News very good this morning. Our troops driving the Huns back and the cavalry have just passed. They look so fine. The Bengal Lancers were among them, so I was told. We're under orders to shift at a moment's notice. It rained heavily this morning. I hope it does not hamper the movements of the cavalry.

If this move ends as successfully as it has begun, it will mean such a lot to the bringing of the war to an end. Our chaps are getting so tired of the mud and

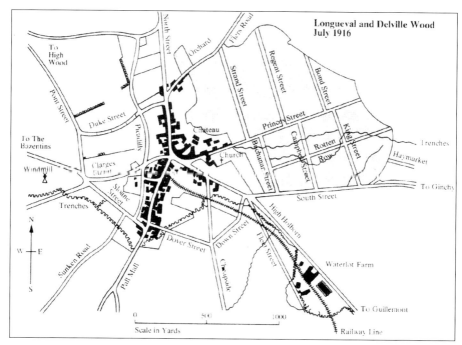

Longueval and Delville Wood – July 1916.

damp. There's such a change in the sunburnt faces of Egypt, and this inactivity makes one as weak as a rat.

The cavalry have done excellent work, now it remains to us infantry to consolidate the positions. We're just ready to move forward. The Bengal Lancers, Canadian cavalry, Scots Greys and Dragoon Guards are all here [In fact the Deccan Horse cavalry had been smashed by German artillery and machine gun fire, which was to spell the end of cavalry on the western front].

Our sergeant mentioned John Forbes, Bob Thompson, Geoghan and myself in his report, for bringing in York[shires] wounded under heavy shell fire. They had been lying out in the open for three days.

Lieutenant-Colonel William Croft commanded the 11th Royal Scots of the 27th Brigade during the attack on Longueval. A resilient Scot, in 1907 he had been wounded by a poisoned arrow while serving in Nigeria. Croft was to be awarded four DSO's during the Great War. He later wrote of the difficulties of taking Longueval:

There were some subterranean passages right through the village of Longueval against which it was rather difficult to compete. The Boche had entrances well on his side of the village, and when things got a bit too warm for him down he would pop like a sewer rat by means of bolt holes in most of the houses.

(*The War Illustrated* Vol VII)

He nearly got the combined battalion headquarters of the Seaforths and [Black] Watch. It was at night, and they were having food, when one of the battalion runners who had been nosing about suddenly rushed in to say that the Boches were next door. As their front line was some considerable way in advance this was particularly cheering intelligence.

2.00pm: The 1st SAI Battalion under Lieut-Col Dawson was sent into Longueval to assist the Scottish regiments. They had had no training in urban warfare, however were to acquit themselves well by using their innate South African sense of firing accurately from shelter. They were subjected to heavy machine-gun fire from the north, north-east and west.

4.00pm: The 1st Battalion A and B Companies reached their objectives. B Company occupied a position west of their objective with A Company on their right flank (east of them); C and D Companies supported them.

Private Henry Sherman, 19, (1st Bn B Coy) from Walmer, Port Elizabeth recalled that his friend, Percy Allen, was shot above the heart and died soon afterwards.

Sergeant Stan Griffiths, 19, and Charles Ingram, 20, were from Uitenhage. Griffiths picked up a wounded man, who was lying in the road, and carried him to safety. His two brothers served with him. Other brothers in B Company were Mandy, Faulds and Pattison.

Lance-Corporal Charles Joseph 'Joey' Pattison (1st Bn B Coy) was originally from Grahamstown, but had worked for the National [Standard] Bank in Mafeking

L/Cpl Joey and Pte Victor Pattison. (Justice K Satchwell)

so joined the 9th Bechuanaland Dismounted Rifles. His younger brother, Victor Reginald, 18, had been with the Southern Rifles and they had both served in Col Berrange's column in German South West Africa.

After being demobilised they enlisted in the 1st Battalion B Company. He later wrote:

> On the morning of the 14th July we left the support trenches at the back of Montauban Wood[?] and advanced as supports to the Seaforths and Black Watch, who had commenced an attack on the Huns in front of Longueval.
>
> We slowly advanced down the shell-blown communication trenches, passing heaps of dead lying just where they were swept down by the German machine-gun fire.
>
> As we pressed on, the sound of heavy fighting grew louder and louder and shells were flying thick all around us, and the air was full of tear-gas, which made tears pour from our eyes and caused great irritation to the lads.
>
> Our objective was Delville Wood which had to be held at all costs. We had to advance up this shell-swept hill and push on past the Scots – clear the village and wood and hang on till relief came.
>
> We were at once extended into line, A Company leading, supported by B, then C, followed by D. Forward we went, shells flying over us, sending down streams of shrapnel, as the Huns knew very well what we were up to; tear-gas filled the air which was shaking and quivering with the deafening noise.

When we arrived a few hundred yards from the village we saw A Company and we all wondered what was wrong. We were not left long in doubt, as we not only came under a barrage of shrapnel but the Germans had spotted us advancing and had every machine-gun they could raise pumping its hail of bullets on us. Men started to drop, the man next to me went down with a piece of shrapnel. How I was not hit I do not know as shrapnel tore up the ground all around me.

We, at once, were given the order to advance at the double and into the village we swept on the heels of A. People talk of Hell. Well, as one lad said, 'Give me Hell every time; they haven't got artillery there'.

In the middle of the village we found the glorious Scots entrenched in a shallow trench, and we jumped in beside them. The order was then sent down, 'All machine- guns cease fire. The South Africans are going to clear Delville Wood'.

Over we charged, C and D Companies swept round to our right and in front of us we could see blue uniforms bolting like rabbits. Well, we cleared the wood, but so deadly was the Huns artillery that we had to fall back to a trench about 100 yards to our rear, and we started digging ourselves in.

Private Frank Maskew, 23, was a Vickers machine-gunner attached to the 1st Battalion:

In all we were in the trenches 20 days, but the first 15 days of this period were pretty mild and we didn't get many casualties. But after that we moved forward and occupied a village [Longueval] and here the rough time began. The enemy had left many snipers and machine-gunners in the village and as we came up many of our chaps were picked off by these and our stretcher-bearers were hard at work.

That day the Huns sent over tear shells by the score, causing us no end of trouble.

Lieutenant Chauncey Reid (1st Bn D Coy) was involved in the house-to-house fighting in the village:

At daybreak we received orders to move, the first battalion leading. We went up round Montauban and reached the other side, where we sat tight for a while in a German communication trench, without casualties.

The rest of the division had attacked Longueval about 3.00am, but whether they had taken it or not, we did not know. About 1 o'clock we were ordered to advance through Longueval to a certain point just inside Delville Wood, and we set out. It was grand. There were tear shells to windward and shrapnel and high explosive all about us. One shrapnel shell burst just above the section I was with and, according to theory, should have wiped out the lot of us, but not one was touched.

The bullets spat round us but none of them hit anything. After that we snapped our fingers at German shrapnel. The tear shells were not at all pleasant, but our masks made them fairly harmless.

Eventually, we got to the outskirts of Longueval and struck the support line of the Black Watch, passed through them and halted for a few moments just beyond. We now really started to get into things. German snipers and machine-guns were having a high old time. On we went again for another hundred yards, and then another halt was called.

I spotted an unfinished German trench and thought it would give excellent cover. So I chased my platoon into it. It was fine – for two seconds. Then, whizz-bang, the Germans opened from our left flank with their eighteen- pounders. They had evidently been waiting for us. We swopped that trench mighty quick for shell holes!

After a pause of ten minutes, we went on to support A and B Companies, which were ahead of us. It was fine! We didn't know the first machine-gun was there until rat-tat-tat, and a couple of men were bowled over. [Lieut Wilfred] Larmuth, who was just in front of me, struck the next one. He crossed a street in time to miss a burst and managed to get half his platoon over with only a couple of casualties. I didn't relish rushing my platoon across at all and, thinking the matter over, contrived to find another way of getting my own lot and the remainder of his across …

(*The War Illustrated* Vol VI)

Longueval was simply a heap of ruins and the machine-guns were impossible to see among the rubble and rubbish. Then we were held up by a crowd of Germans in a house. Larmuth, being in front, was sent out with a bombing party to clear them out, and returned two minutes later to report that the bombing party had been blotted out instead. Again he was sent out and the same thing happened.

Then he was sent round one way with his platoon, and I was sent another way with mine, so as to hold up an encircling movement on our right. I reached the place with very few casualties and, after digging in, received orders to hang on until the 2nd or 3rd Regiments came through.

Private James Yeatman 'Boysie' Nash, 26, from Steytlerville had served with the First Eastern Rifles in South West Africa. According to L/Cpl Joey Pattison.

Boysie Nash. (P Kirkman)

I never saw anything so plucky in all my life as the way Nash led his little party. The word was given, 'Charge', and over he jumped, followed by the lads, and charged right up at the Huns ahead. He ran too fast, not looking back to see if his men could keep up – with the result that he got to the German parapet before the Huns were aware of his approach, and the last we saw of Nash was a stalwart figure blazing away with his rifle on top of the Huns' parapet – then he fell forward and disappeared, and what was left of his lads had to retire under the hail of bombs.

Private A Vaughan from Port Elizabeth was one of his eight comrades who had to withdraw. He later graphically described seeing Nash fall on the German trench parapet, 20 yards off. [Nash is buried in Grave XK1 in the Delville Wood Cemetery].

Gordon Smith (1st Bn B Coy) later wrote:

We all had to run the gauntlet of death that morning. It was a case of trust to luck & the speed you ran at. There was an open space between the houses about 60 yards wide.

We all had to double across this space to be able to outflank the enemy. Firing at us from the right was one sniper and from the left at about 30 yards range there were six or eight snipers & one machine-gun. I doubled across without being hit, following me was Dick [Richard Carter]. He got across safely.

Then Lance Cpl Atkinson. He got two bullets through the left arm and one in the right thigh. Then came Percy Allen. We saw him reel just before he reached safety which at this point was a brick wall. He staggered into safety just in time & then dropped between about six of us. We worked hard trying to staunch the wound from which the blood was flowing in a stream. The bullet went in just above the heart & came out at the back between the shoulder blades.

Percival (Percy) Joseph Allen was to die of his wounds in hospital on 19 July. His brother Sec/Lieut Alfred (Bertie) Allen of the Highland Light Infantry was killed at Delville Wood on 16 July.

6.00pm: An attack on the 'Chateau' failed. It lay between the village and wood and was heavily defended. Tunnels probably ran from its basement into the wood and to village strong points.

8.35pm: Lieutenant Reid received a message from Major Edward Burges, 38:

Lieut Reid. I am withdrawing to the left flank to support Capt Miller. The colonel [Dawson] wishes you to stay where you are – pending the attack by 2nd and 3rd, as promised to Lieut Roseby. Should these regiments pass, you will endeavour to join me as soon as possible.

Reid was not to know that Operational Order 48 would be changed and that the 2nd and 3rd would not advance until the next morning.

We hadn't been there half an hour when I heard that Larmuth and Dent had been wounded [Lieut Wilfred Larmuth was wounded by British artillery fire whereas Lieut William Dent had his right arm shattered].

We had just taken up our position when the Germans advanced along a communication trench running from about twenty yards to our right into the lines to which they had been driven back. Luckily, the Seaforths came up from behind and a lively fight was waged – chiefly bombs and machine-guns being used. It was pretty warm while it lasted, but a Stokes gun finished Mr Hun.

When I got time to look round I found that behind us were about a dozen German dugouts and, as it struck me that there might be Germans inside, I decided to clear them. There were thirteen Germans in the first. The Black Watch took them back. You never saw such a scared crowd in all your life. One poor little German nearly had a bayonet in his ribs because he prayed instead of putting his hands up!

I took two men with me to clear the next dugout [on the southern edge of Delville Wood], but the Huns wouldn't come out. One of my men spoke German and told them that, if they didn't surrender, we would blow them out, but they either didn't understand or were afraid of bayonets and preferred to stay below.

(*The War Illustrated* Vol VII)

I threw in one of their own bombs, just to shake 'em up a bit and intending to go down after it, before any who were left could recover. And that is all I know of the fight …

The dugout, as I have since discovered, was evidently a grenade store, and the whole affair blew up, taking me and one of my men with it …

Private Jack Carstens (1st Bn D Coy) found his platoon fighting without an officer. Lieut Nimmo Brown was dead and his No 16 Platoon was commanded by Sgt Ginger King:

We spent some time in and around Longueval village – a most unpleasant spot with continuous sniping from all quarters. On one occasion we were passing through a wrecked garden with a small gate at its end. One at a time we had to pass through and make a bolt across the road for the comparative safety of a ruined building. We had to wait for the officer's order: 'Run!' and then each made his dash. The fellow in front of me was unlucky. He was killed in mid-flight.

It was now my turn. I opened the gate and was about to run when an explosion occurred uncomfortably close to my ear. A piece of the gate had been shot away and I turned to 'Moeg' Carey immediately behind clutching his face in pain. Taking his hands away I could see that his lower jaw had been blown to pieces. As he moved away to find a stretcher bearer I had time to tap him on the shoulder and wish him luck before the officer called my run. In a second or two I was safely over …

After I had left him he was found by a medical orderly as he sat stunned behind an old ruin. And the first thing the orderly offered him was a slab of chocolate – a man with a shattered jaw offered a slab of chocolate! However he was tough enough to survive it all and even in those days plastic surgery must have been pretty good for he was able to take up his oil company job where he left it, and has only a scar or two to show for his ordeal.

It was during that same episode in Longueval Village that Bill Carlson was killed. Many of the old generation must remember this great sportsman who played centre-three-quarter [fly-half] for Villagers and cricket for the Alma Club.

Our little party were sheltering behind that ruin across the road and awaiting further orders from the officer, who so far had not appeared [as he was a casualty!]. We spotted the enemy in a trench not fifty yards down the road. For a handful of men, without an officer or even an NCO, to attack and possibly fall into a trap seemed out of the question.

But not for Bill; and he could not resist the temptation of pitching into the enemy forthwith. I'm perfectly certain that he imagined himself back on the rugger battlefield of Newlands and he had to cross that line.

I can see him now with a Mills bomb in his hand careering down the main street of Longueval. None of our shouts would stop him. On he went. On – until a machine-gunner from the top of one of the ruined buildings let fly. He was riddled with bullets and never moved again.

I am happy to think that our recommendation for the Military Medal for Bill Carlson was accepted but nothing could make up for the gap that was left in our little intimate group of sportsmen who had left for the wars together.

Lieutenant Chauncey Reid was dragged from the shattered dugout and carried to the aid shelter, where he recovered consciousness:

The first thing I remember was the Padre [Hill] asking me whether I would like a sip of Bovril. Whether I actually got it, or not, I don't know. The next time I came to I was being shoved into a dugout somewhere out of the way of shells. We were obviously going through the German barrage.

Lance-Corporal Joey Pattison (1st Bn B Coy) continued:

It was now evening, and a very heavy rain had set in. We were soaked to the skin, hungry and exposed to the most ghastly shell fire. All round us lay our comrades and pals of the past 12 months, stretched out in their last sleep, but they had not died in vain, because the Germans lay in heaps everywhere.

As the sun set in front of us, we saw the Huns advancing, feeling their way with an occasional bomb. We quickly got all our bombs ready and remained quite still, and as soon as they got within range, they had the surprise of their lives, and when the heavy smoke had cleared away, only the heaps of dead Germans gave evidence that their attempted counter-attack had failed.

We then set to and got ourselves dug in as deep as possible, as the Germans had dug themselves in just out of bombing range and their snipers were dropping our lads right and left.

So far dear old Vic and I had been lucky, and we set to and made a ripping dug-out to shelter us from the rain. Nothing was shelter from the shells, as was evident when our pals came past one by one – others being carried by stretcher-bearers.

Well, darkness arrived with all its horrors, voices crying piteously for stretcher-bearers, and some lads we had left in the wood ahead of us whom we could not assist till it got darker.

14 July – Germans at the Second Line

The 16th (Bavarian) Infantry Regiment [IR16] from near Munich had been earmarked to relieve the badly mauled Reserve Infantry Regiment 99 at Thiepval on 30 June, but was instead brought forward to Flers. I Bn arrived at 2.25pm on 1 July and took up position on the northern side of the village. At 3.40pm III Bn followed and went to ground near the cemetery.

II Bn was ordered to defend the line Bazentin le Grand to Longueval. It was known that 14 July was the French National Day, celebrating the storming of the Bastille in 1789. It was presumed that the British would honour their allies by launching a massive attack on the second line that morning.

The four companies of II Bn were deployed as follows: the 5th and 6th along the south and south-east edges of Longueval with the 7th at almost a right angle to the Sugar Factory (Waterlot-Farm). The 8th Company held the strongpoint's in Longueval.

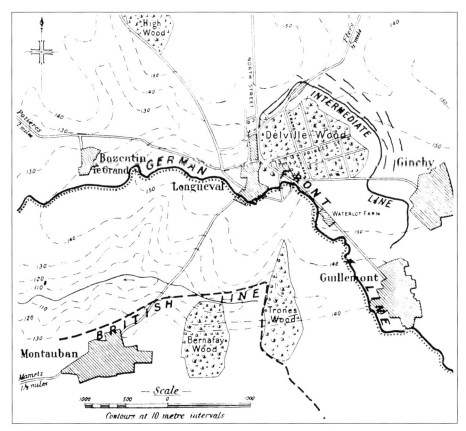

The German Brown Line – Braune Stellung – on 13 July 1916. (*Army Quarterly* 1925)

During the dawn attack on the 14th the Scottish regiments hurled themselves at the German positions and were met by a withering fire. Major Killermann, II/16, had ordered his troops to be prepared for a night attack.

Extracts from the German Official History records the ensuing bloodbath:

In the early hours (2.25am) of the 14th the enemy attacked mainly on the front held by the 5th and 6th Companies, on the south-west and south-east edges of Longueval. As soon as the 5th Coy sentries noticed the approach of the enemy, the alarm was raised and the men stormed out of their cover. Lt dR Thurnreiter on the right wing fired a star-shell. By its light the close columns of plucky Scottish troops could be seen approaching the remains of the wire entanglement, flame-throwers to the fore.

The 5th Coy commander, Oblt dR Weber stood with his men, firing and hurling hand grenades at the approaching enemy. The machine-gun on the left wing mowed down the rows of approaching Scots, who repeatedly attempted to break through at the sunken road from Montauban to Longueval.

Within ten minutes the enemy had been repulsed in the front lines. However, it was realized that the enemy had broken through between the left wing of I Bn and the right wing of II Bn, so a platoon under Lt dR Thurnreiter was sent to block the position. Within a short time the hand grenade throwing enemy appeared only some 15 to 20 meters away behind the rear of the 5th Coy. Simultaneously new waves of enemy troops approached from the front, but were repulsed. The right wing was heavily fired on by enemy machine-guns. As the ammunition depot had been buried, the resultant lack of ammunition caused a gradual loss of fire power.

Isolated Scots approached with shouted orders to surrender, but the Bavarians had retained sufficient ammunition to repulse these approaches decisively. The machine-gun on the left wing was then silenced by the enemy, who had broken through with strong forces at the point of contact between the 5th and 6th Coys, on the road Maricourt-Longueval, and was beginning to roll up the 5th Coy positions.

Fighting was extremely heavy. Leutnant dR Otto Drechsler was killed and his second in-command, Sgt Bren was seriously wounded. Although covered in blood, Vize-feldwebel Wimmer dashed to the company commander and reported the serious position on the left wing. Everyone was calling for ammunition. Oblt dR Weber vainly demanded help from the troops in the rear. Gefr Geiger requested permission to return to the battalion headquarters to report the serious position of the 5th Coy, but had hardly retired three metres when he was killed.

The Scots then brought a light trench mortar forward. Soon shells and hand grenades assailed the positions. Close formations of Scots ran forward shouting: "Come on!" Helpless without ammunition, some 40 men clustered about their company commander, Lt dR Thurnreiter and Utffz Bauer, the only remaining unwounded officer.

Oberleutnant dR Weber, deciding not to sacrifice his men without reason, called: 'Men, you have defended yourselves bravely! We surrender for the Fatherland'. The enemy closed in swiftly and an English officer came forward praising the bravery of the Bavarians who had held on to the last so tenaciously. They had fought their last fight and were led off into honourable captivity.

About 3.45am the forward sections of Longueval were subjected to a half-hour of extremely heavy drum-fire. Major Killermann ordered that the 8th Coy ready themselves for defence of the village. The company commander, Oblt Schwub, immediately sent his men into the battle.

It was still pitch dark and the village was under a heavy bombardment. Nothing could be distinguished and there seemed to be no let up in the heavy enemy fire. In addition, curtain fire from the 3rd Guards Div increased the incredible noise of the battle.

A French village under bombardment. (Ditsong National Museum of Military History)

As the telephone lines were destroyed no news from the battlefronts was forthcoming. The morning then dawned. At last Oblt Schwub managed to get a runner through with a message: "Enemy has penetrated the I/16 position west of Longueval and is over the road Longueval-Bazentin le Grand. Company is holding the right flank position and repulsing the enemy."

Leutnant Heindl with 30 men was in a trench in the sunken road west of Longueval when attacked. After heavy fighting the enemy was repulsed. Leutnant Heindl personally rescued two badly wounded men who were lying out in the open, though he was himself wounded. He and his men then successfully repulsed a further enemy attack.

In order to have a better view of the enemy, Lt Heindl climbed a tree and directed his machine-gunner onto a strong enemy detachment which was on the right flank, north of the Bazentin le Grand road. The enemy suffered heavy casualties and was scattered.

Meanwhile Major Killermann had received a message from the 8th Coy: "Enemy has penetrated the south part of Longueval and has got as far as the barricaded position, where they have been stopped. Battle still in progress. Company is holding the barricade position, but coy commander wounded". The sound of small arms fire could be heard from that direction. The barricade position was south of the road from Bazentin le Grand to Longueval and divided it into two sections.

II/6 was now fighting in two separate groups, which surprisingly enough the Scottish troops did not take advantage of. Major Killermann attempted to inform the 7th Coy of the position in Longueval and of the state the 8th Coy was in, but his runners were killed by enemy fire from Longueval and Delville Wood. At about 9.00am he moved his command post from the difficult terrain in the northern part of Longueval to Point 140 on the road to Flers.

A platoon of the 6/26 was sent to reinforce the weakest point of the 8th Bavarian Coy, where Lt Heindl with only 10 men still held on. Though badly weakened through loss of blood from his leg wound, he had insisted on remaining until his position had been completely handed over to the IR 26.

Leutnant dR Hans Drechsler was conspicuous in controlling the defences in Longueval, arranging for machine-guns to be fetched and in rallying the remnants of the 8th Coy. At about 2.00pm Major Killermann received an order: "All remaining Bavarian troops to assemble in Beaulencourt." Men who retired to Flers found the order to be incorrect. Killermann had not believed the order, so had not passed it on to the 7th Coy.

The 7th Coy had incurred heavy losses but continued fighting in Longueval. When their ammunition ran low they used the weapons of dead Scots. At 6.00pm the commander, Oblt Scheuring, requested artillery support from Ginchy but was advised that all the guns were destroyed. In order not to needlessly sacrifice his men he ordered a retreat at 8.15pm.

Under cover of a machine-gun group they managed to retire without too many losses, via the Sugar Factory to Ginchy. Through Oblt Scheuring's tenacious defence in the south of Longueval, enough time was gained for fresh troops to enter from the north.

The IR 16 paid dearly for the time it bought; the regiment lost 72 officers and 2,559 men. It reassembled with eight officers and 688 men. Genmaj Von Lindequest wrote a letter of thanks to Genmaj Burkhard on 16 July, praising the bravery and tenacity of the men. Oberleutnant Scheuring, Lt Heindl and Lt dR Hans Drechsler were later to be decorated with the Bavarian Military 'Max Joseph' Order.

German Artillery

One of the German artillerists in action that day, Anno Noack, 25, was a Silesian coalminer, originally from Aachen. At the time he was ADC to the commander of the German light artillery in that section of the front. His day was to begin with a shock:

> One of your bombs which rained down on us in preparation of your attack on Delville Wood smashed the entrance to my dugout. As our battery was behind the fighting line I was sent to direct the fire of our artillery and investigate the position.

Lieut Anno Noack of the German Artillery. (Mrs A Noack)

Fortunately for us … I could report as a result of my reconnaissance that the advance of the enemy had been stopped, partly owing to the fall of night. In fact your infantry had broken through our foremost ranks.

General Von Falkenhayn had issued instructions not to yield an inch. *Nur über Leichen darf der Feind seinen Weg vorwärts finden* [The enemy must not be allowed to advance except over corpses]. When offered quarter by a body of Highlanders a German officer replied, "I and my men have orders to defend this position with our lives. German soldiers know how to obey orders. We thank you for your offer, but we die where we stand." And they did.

The 6th Recruit Coy of the 9th Grenadiers was ordered forward from east Flers to assist in clearing Longueval. Two platoons advanced through heavy artillery fire to Delville Wood. While moving through the wood they were fired on from the south side. They reached Longueval and joined the IR 26.

Generalstabschef Erich von Falkenhayn. (I Weisser)

At 9.00am on 14 July the IR 26 (Magdeburgers), from east of Berlin, were ordered by the 8th Infantry Division to retake the three kilometre line between Bazentin le Petit and Longueval.

It's commander, Oberst Paul Grautoff, 47, was born in Lauban, in the Prussian province of Silesia, on 31 December, 1868. At age eighteen he joined the Prussian army, then studied at the military academy from 1895-8. From 1910 he served with German colonial troops in German South West Africa. Grautoff returned to Germany in October 1913 to command a light infantry battalion. In January 1914 he was promoted lieut-colonel.

When World War I began Grautoff joined the General Staff of the 1st Army then commanded the Oldenburgischen Infantry Regiment No 91 in France. In January 1915 he became Chief of

Genmaj Grautoff. (IR 26 History)

the General Staff of Lines of Communication of the Southern Army. Thereafter he commanded the 1st Magdeburgers Infantry Regiment 26 at the Somme.

The IR 26 I and III Bns took the village of Bazentin le Petit and won ground towards Bazentin le Grand. Later in the day, due to lack of artillery support, they were forced to retire.

At 2.00pm the German IR 16 (Bavarians) Regt was reinforced by the IR 26 (Magdeburgers). On the left flank, II Bn went to ground in the northern part of Longueval, where they found weak remnants of IR 16 Bavarians. Their 8th Company reached the southern perimeter of Delville Wood but had to retreat after the loss of all officers.

Meanwhile II Bn of IR 163 (Schleswig-Holstein), from near the Danish border, were brought up to support II Bn of IR 26.

The Germans withdrew from Trônes Wood into the Brown Line, their losses having been too heavy to hold the forward positions. In the meantime the British had launched a massive attack against Longueval and Delville Wood, which increasingly posed a threat to the III/106 positioned on the Brown Line north of Guillemont.

RIR 107 Arrive

On 14 July the Reserve Infantry Regiment 107 was ordered by the 12th Reserve Division to march to Sailly, and to take up reserve positions there. Late in the afternoon the regiment was ordered into attack positions in front of Trônes Wood and along the Brown Line.

Resting during the march to the
Somme – 13 July 1916.
(RIR 107 History)

Their commander was Oberst Karl Adam Ludwig von Wuthenau, 53. He had been born in Dresden on 26 June, 1863, a descendant of the aristocratic Wuthenau family. His mother had been born Countess of Wurttenberg. After studying jurisprudence at a Bonn university he joined the Prussian army, did an officer's course and served in the 1st Guards Dragoon Regiment in Berlin in 1885, then in the Ulanen Regiment Nr 21.

His father was elevated to a Prussian earldom in October 1911 as Earl of Wuthenau-Hohenthurm. He was promoted major in 1912 and given command of the 2nd Ulanen Regiment Nr 18. In December 1913 Von Wuthenau was promoted lieut-colonel in command of the regiment. In January 1914 he became a Reserve Officer.

He married Marie Antoinette Countess Chotek von Chotkowa and Wognin (1874-1930) and they had two daughters and four sons. Her sister, Sophia, married Archduke Franz Ferdinand, the heir to Francis Joseph of Austria.

On 28 June 1914, Von Wuthenau's sister-in-law and her husband were murdered in Sarajevo, which was the spark which set off the train of events leading to the outbreak of the First World War.

Von Wuthenau was recalled to serve as a colonel of the Reserve Infantry Regiment 107. He was to lead this regiment on the Somme

Oberst Graf von Wuthenau.
(RIR 107 History)

where he distinguished himself through personal bravery at Delville Wood and at Guillemont. His regiment's history stated:

> Before the RIR 107 could consolidate their position before Delville Wood, the British stormed from Trônes Wood, past the Sugar Factory and took parts of Delville Wood. At midnight the regiment was ordered to take up positions between Delville Wood and Ginchy in order to secure the right flank of the division. Despite a heavy enemy bombardment, by the morning the regiment had almost succeeded in digging a continuous trench east of the wood.

Summary of Events – Friday 14 July 1916

(Time is given as British time. German time was approximately an hour earlier).

3.25am: 9th Div 26th and 27th Bdes attack Longueval village. Survivors of the IR 16 hold northern Longueval.

9.00am: IR 26 ordered to retake the Bazentines and Longueval. II/163 brought up to support II/26 in the village.

2.00pm: The 1st SAI Bn reinforces the 26th and 27th Bdes in Longueval. The IR 16 are reinforced by the IR 26.

6.00pm: Col Dawson of the 1st SAI orders an attack on 'The Chateau', which fails.

5

The Wood – Saturday 15 July

12.55am: Orders were received that the 1st SA Infantry Brigade was to attack Delville Wood.

2.40am: The 9th Division requested that two companies [B and C] of the 4th Battalion be detached to support them. A platoon from each assisted the 5th Cameron Highlanders of the 26th Brigade in taking Waterlot Farm. A and D Companies were ordered to advance on Delville Wood.

(*Deeds that Thrill the Empire*)

4.00am: The 2nd and 3rd Battalions reached the support trench east of Longueval. At 6.00am most of the brigade advanced into Delville Wood. Sharpshooters were sent ahead to clear the wood as best they could.

Lance-Corporal Joey Pattison (1st Bn B Coy) woke early:

> Well, we all welcomed the morning, and found that our C and D companies had moved forward and occupied a more advanced position which protected our company from a frontal attack, but we still had the Hun very much on our left flank. Well, we held these positions for five weary days and nights, being slowly picked off one by one by their deadly snipers, and the terrible shell fire.

Private Sherman (1st Bn B Coy) recalled:

> 'Dad' MacDonald brought down several snipers before himself being killed. Willie Ferguson, the baker's son, also fell. The Company dug in facing the north-west side of the wood, which was heavily defended by the Germans.

Private Gordon Smith (1st Bn B Coy) wrote,

> During that time the Huns made several attacks on us, preceded by heavy bombardments with tear-gas shells (which blind you for some hours, but which are otherwise harmless), shrapnel, high explosive shells, Coal Boxes (a shell, high explosive & weighing about 1500 P[ound]s) & last, but not least, liquid fire. None of their attacks however were successful, rather were they the reverse, as we wiped out large numbers of the Huns.
>
> Of course, the bombardments which preceded their attacks, accounted for some of our men, but our casualties were as nothing compared to theirs. It's their own fault too, as they will persist in attacking in massed formation. Just imagine what a target they present to our chaps who are every one, good shots. Anyhow, massed formation is a good idea, for us. The more they advance that way the better we like it & the more we kill & the more we kill the sooner the war will end.

Private Jack Carstens (1st Bn D Coy) was suspicious.

> And now the appointed time for our attack on Delville Wood had arrived. I was only a private soldier, with the tactics of the High Command all unknown to me. But, as a private soldier it was – and still is – my conviction that the German High Command invited us into the Wood.
>
> I can only speak of the experience I had with my company of the 1st South African Infantry. We took up our positions and marched into the Wood in column of line. Everything was perfectly quiet and still. I even noticed the birds

flitting from tree to tree. To the soldier next to me I remarked: 'This is easy. I wonder where the Hun is hiding.'

8.00am: The 3rd Battalion occupied the wood south of Princes Street.

By 9.00am the 2nd Battalion had advanced up Strand Street and reached the northern perimeter. B Company was left holding Strand Street despite losing its two captains. Harold Creed was killed while Billy Barlow was shell-shocked and wounded. Lieutenant Walter Hill, 35, and Sec-Lieut Errol Tatham, 25, both from Pietermaritzburg, remained.

Errol Tatham led his men in close-quarter fighting and drove the Germans back. He tried to ensure that a former Boer officer, Nicholas Vlok, 49, who had been wounded, received attention. Vlok was later assaulted by a large German, who was summarily bayoneted by a passing South African.

Walter Hill's platoon ran out of ammunition and had to surrender. They were escorted out of the wood, then Hill attacked their guard, grabbed his weapon and fought his way back into the wood, followed by some of his men.

The Border men in the Natal Battalion headed for the northern side of the wood. Second-Lieutenant Arthur Knibbs (2nd Bn D Coy) from East London was in for a rude shock.

(*The War Illustrated* Vol VII)

The Bosche spotted us before we had even been there ten minutes, and oh what a time he gave us. We started driving them out of the wood immediately and in an hour we had them out. Their snipers did a lot of damage; they were well hidden up the trees. That night they tried a counter-attack, but we gave them a warm time with our machine-guns. Whenever it was quiet we dug holes and connected them, making a trench of it.

11.15am: The 1st Battalion returned to Lieut-Col Tanner's command. D Company was sent to the northern edge of the wood and ordered to dig in. Private Jack Carstens recalled:

Lieut Walter Hill.
(Major W Speirs and Mrs D Nel)

(*The War Illustrated*
Vol VI)

Arriving at the end of the Wood, a ploughed field in front of us, our orders to
dig in on its fringe. We carried picks and shovels for that purpose but I was never
much good at that game and found the ground unbelievably hard and myself
desperately tired. I noticed that one of the fellows had already finished his funk
hole – a husky fellow, with obviously a lot of pick and shovel work in his history.
'Robbie,' I cried, 'dig me a funk hole and I'll give you five francs.' That hole was
dug and I was in it, in a matter of minutes …

Shortly after, little hell was let loose. It seemed as though the Germans had
brought every available gun from the whole Western Front for the express
purpose of blasting the South Africans out of Delville Wood.

Private Frank Maskew (1st Bn M-G) and his Vickers machine-gun team also
moved.

By the next day [Saturday 15th] we had the village pretty well cleared of all Huns
and that night we occupied a wood in front of the village. Dead Germans were
lying thick here and also many of our own fellows.

Private James Simpson (4th Bn M-G) found it difficult moving through the wood
to the northern perimeter:

(*The War Illustrated* Vol VIII)

Shells whistled through the trees and burst with awful cracks all around. Men were falling fast, and everyone was calling for the stretcher-bearers. To add to the confusion all the fellows were carrying extra loads of ammunition boxes, rolls of barbed wire, tins of water and a hundred and one other things.

We in the gun section each had to carry two canvas buckets of Lewis-gun magazines besides our rifle and equipment and I can tell you every time we trekked the perspiration simply ran off me and then came the shivers when we halted.

We struggled through the wood, being tripped up almost every step by the thick undergrowth, barbed wire, and falls into shell holes or else our equipment would get entangled in the brambles. The boys were falling right and left.

Private Joe Samuels, 18, (3rd Bn A Coy) had enlisted in the Rand Rifles when aged 16, after lying about his age, and served in South West Africa. He recalled that on entering Delville Wood:

We were ordered to whisper when moving in with fixed bayonets. I saw a soldier in grey, but he darted away. Was he French or German? I didn't know, but we moved forward 100 yards then began firing. We took cover and it went on all day. The Germans counter-attacked and shelled. I was wounded later and carried out on a stretcher.

11.30am: Elements of the 3rd Battalion B and D Companies, under Captains Richard Medlicott MC and Leonard Tomlinson, attacked the Germans east of the wood. They had been unsure of the identity of the troops opposing them and some men had climbed trees to confirm that the strangers wore coalscuttle helmets.

The attack was a resounding success, killing 32 and capturing three officers and 135 men. While shepherding the prisoners to the wood they were fired on and some of the prisoners were killed.

12.00pm: The German RIR 107 (Saxons) II and III Battalions attacked the north-east perimeter. The men of the 2nd and 3rd Battalion D Companies opened fire at 600 yards but the Germans closed to 50 yards before the 4th Battalion A and D Companies reinforced them, using craters and hastily dug trenches as cover. The Germans then dug in 80 yards from the wood, having lost 28 officers and 500 men.

2.00pm: Lieut-Col Tanner reported to Gen Lukin that he held virtually the whole wood, but that one of his companies had virtually ceased to exist [2nd Bn B Coy]. He was under attack and requested reinforcements, so the 4th Battalion's D Coy was sent to his assistance. Lieutenant Sandy Young VC then had his right hand shattered by a whizz-bang, so joined the walking wounded in retracing their steps.

Private Eddie Fitz (2nd Bn HQ) was the son of an American sea captain from Portland, Maine, who had been left behind ill when his ship sailed from the Kowie

River mouth. Eddie Fitz was schooled in East London and served in the Kaffrarian Rifles before joining the brigade.

He was a signaller who for two days at Bernafay Wood with two companions, L/Cpl Fred Mitchell and Pte Robert Douthwaite, kept re-connecting the telephone wires during the shelling. For this they were to earn the brigade's first Military Medals. Lieut-Col Tanner decided rather to use runners than telephone wires in Delville Wood, so Fitz found himself free to assist in other ways.

> We were instructed under a sergeant to go scrounging for ammunition. We scrounged all about and went into Longueval, into a temporary dressing station we found there and we all came back, strapped around the neck with eight or ten khaki bandoliers – loaded with them.
>
> Then we had to distribute them down to our companies and we were sniped at. I didn't shoot anybody. I wasn't in a position to do much as we were occupied. In the normal course of events I would have had to be running lines.
>
> My real buddy, Les Mandy, was with me. All the way from Armentières we stuck together. Early in the afternoon, after the ammunition stint, six or eight of us were gathered in a helluva big shell hole, just waiting for instructions. As we moved down to this area there was a burst of machine-gun fire. I suppose they saw us coming. Les fell, shot through the chest. We took him into the shell hole …
>
> We were told to just disperse around headquarters and dig ourselves in – just to get ourselves below ground. A chap named Henry Oldfield and I did so. We only had trenching tools – no spades. We chopped out and put the stuff over.
>
> A shell hit a tree above us and exploded and we got some of the down-draft from it. He got a piece past his head and in the shoulder muscle. It stuck in the back of his shoulder blade. He was moaning about this thing, but we decided the only thing to do was to keep digging and get ourselves properly down.
>
> I said to him, 'You know this trench is muddy. It's getting water. How can this be?' Anyhow it proved to be that my hand was bleeding. No bones were broken but the flesh was torn open. So in the light of a match he got hold of a dressing and dressed my hand up.

Lieutenant-Colonel Tanner became aware of the heroism of one of his officers (see pages 92-3) and was later to write:

> In the fighting in the thick wood in the northern part of Delville Wood on 15th July 1916, Lieutenant W J Hill, 2nd SAI, and a small party of men were surrounded by a stray party of the enemy and after a stubborn resistance (during which numbers of the party were killed or wounded) were rushed and made prisoners and despatched to the enemy end of the wood and there placed by twos and threes in different shell holes under armed guards.

Lieutenant Hill, watching his opportunity suddenly attacked and overpowered the guard over his shell hole at the greatest risk to himself, for had he not succeeded in killing or rendering unconscious the guard, numbers of the enemy within easy hailing distance would have undoubtedly instantly appeared. Lieutenant Hill then led his few men, under heavy fire, back to our lines ...

4.40pm: The Germans attacked the northern flank from the Flers Road. They were beaten off by a high rate of fire.

Private Cyril Weldon (1st Bn D Coy) was in charge of a Lewis-gun, which did devastating work when they came up in support of Natal's 2nd Bn A Company.

6.00pm: A further attack from the Flers Road was repulsed. The German rate of shell fire then increased after dusk. The remainder of the 1st Battalion was then sent into the wood from the village.

Walter Giddy (2nd Bn D Coy) recorded their fight on the north-eastern perimeter:

15th. We went into Delville Wood and drove the Huns out of it, and entrenched ourselves on the edge, losing many men, but we drove them off, as they would come back and counter attack. Their snipers were knocking our fellows over wholesale, while we were digging trenches, but our chaps kept them off. I got behind a tree, just with my right eye and shoulder showing, and blazed away.

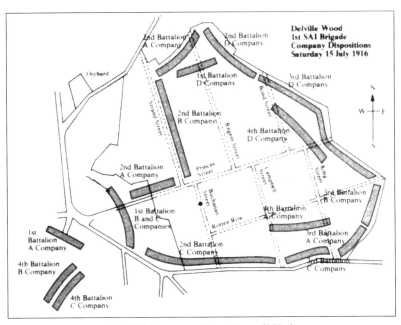

1st SAI Company dispositions. (I Uys)

The Seaforths Pioneer B Company reported to the OC 2nd Bn D Company, for whom they began digging support trenches.

7.00pm: Major Hunt's two companies of the 4th Bn (B and C) were ordered to construct a strong-point. Brigadier Lukin sent Lieut Percy Roseby, 39, to ascertain the position in the wood. Private Sherman (1st Bn B Coy) said,

> That night they made a strong counter-attack, but we beat them off. The row was beyond description, and we fired where we thought they were.

German dispositions

12.35am: The German IR 72 (Thüringian) Regiment left the Bapaume area to march to Delville Wood.

On the northern perimeter, according to IR 163 (Holsteiners):

> At daybreak on 15 July patrols of II/163 discovered enemy troops in Delville Wood. The British [South Africans] had succeeded by using the unoccupied eastern perimeter of the wood in advancing to the northern perimeter and digging in with four machine-guns, which then controlled the Flers-Longueval road.
>
> The 9th Company under Lt Krohn then advanced with orders to clear the northern perimeter of the wood. During the advance the company suffered heavy casualties. As Leutnant Krohn was wounded, Lt Bahr took command. The company could not carry out its orders entirely as the enemy consisted of a very strong troop of at least company strength.
>
> The wood was also heavily overgrown so that advance was very difficult. The 9th company attacked and Lt Bahr was killed. Since any further advance on the British was hopeless, the company remained in position until evening. Parts of IR 153 came to reinforce the company and in darkness this strengthened troop was able to clear the enemy positions from the west.
>
> During the night hand grenade attacks by the British [sic] were repulsed. Strong artillery fire straddled the whole section so that it was not possible to improve emplacements.

Eastern Perimeter

On the eastern side of Delville Wood Oberst Von Wuthenau's RIR 107 awaited the expected assault in their newly-dug trenches.

> By 9.00am on the morning of 15 July the enemy bombardment had risen to such intensity that an attack seemed imminent.
>
> At 11.30am British troops [South African 3rd Bn B and D Coys] suddenly broke out of Delville Wood and within moments had taken large numbers of the

Ehrenstein-Riebel Battalion, formed from the remnants of single battalions of IR 23 and IR 38, prisoner.

The Midday Assault

In order to regain Longueval and Delville Wood, the German 8th Infantry Division had decided on an attack from the north to be supported by the 12th Reserve Division, of which RIR 107 was a part.

The II and III Battalions of RIR 107 were ordered to join this attack from Flers under the leadership of Major Eckhardt. At 12.30 pm the battalions stormed forward in four waves against Delville Wood, coming to within 400 metres of the edge. Here, however, heavy enemy artillery and machine-gun fire caused the battalions heavy losses and slowed down the attack.

The II Battalion commander, Major Von der Decken, was killed instantly, and within a short period of time the battalion had lost almost all its officers. Nevertheless the men managed to carry the attack to within 80m of the wood. Here they came to a stop and in the face of heavy enemy fire the remains of the battalions dug in.

Two companies of the I/104 and a further company of the III/107 that had been held back as reserve were now also thrown into the battle for Delville Wood. In support of the III/107 they managed to advance a little, but their losses were so heavy that they were pulled back into the sunken Ginchy-Flers road, leaving the II/107 to hold its position.

German troops before an attack. (I Weisser)

Although brigade messages reported that the attack from the north was going well, no relief was noticed in the sections held by the RIR 107. A further attack ordered for midnight was cancelled when the enemy began a particularly heavy bombardment on the attack area. Losses in both battalions up to this point were eight officers and 106 men dead, 20 officers and 478 men wounded.

Meanwhile Sixt von Armin's 8th Div was brought from south of Bapaume as reinforcements. It included the IR 153 and IR 72, who were to significantly affect the fighting in the area.

The IR 153 (Altenburgers) arrive

During the morning of the 15th, III/153 was placed under command of IR 26 (7th ID), which was in position to the right of the 8th ID. II/153 with the remaining Machine-Gun Company under Major Von Stosch was brought forward into the sunken road north of Flers as reserve.

The IR 72 (Thüringians) arrive

On 13 July the regiment was south-east of Douai, on the 14th west of Cambrai and on the 15th south-east of Bapaume:

> The troops were not used to marching anymore, so in this way were brought forward gradually in night marches of 10 km, 15 km and 25 km into the Somme area.
>
> The battle area could be recognised from a great distance; dozens of fixed balloons floated above it and the dull roar of an unbelievably heavy bombardment, never before experienced in this measure, was an indication of the hell on earth awaiting the regiment. The regiment was commanded by Major Zander in place of Oberst Von Doetinchen.
>
> On 15 July at 12.35am the regiment was ordered to march to Gueudecourt where at 4.00am they were to be ready to advance further ...
>
> The 6th, 7th and 8th companies advanced in line toward the Foureaux Wedge (The High Wood/Longueval gap) objective, the 5th Coy following. They reached the position without hindrance, from where the 8th Coy under command of its courageous leader, Lt dR Penzler, advanced without resistance to find remnants of the Reserve Battalion 55, Infantry Regiment 163, Grenadier Regiment 9 and Infantry Regiment 26 in the front-line.
>
> The 8th Company was able to send conclusive information on the front line position from Hill 140 (the northernmost point of Delville Wood) back to the regimental command post at about 9.00am, the first reliable information which they received.
>
> Towards midday the 6th and 7th Companies followed the 8th into the front-line, but were subjected to a heavy bombardment with resultant heavy losses. All

troops then in the position between the north-east corner of Foureaux Wood and the Western exit of Longueval were placed under the command of the regiment. The 6th Company, however, was placed under the command of Oberstlt Grautoff of IR 26, as this company had already advanced beyond the road into Delville Wood.

The enemy artillery bombardment kept up all day and the night in steady intensity and the companies suffered heavy losses. The 6th Company (with IR 26) had already lost all of its officers. Lt dR Schultz was killed leading his platoon, Lt dR Seehous was critically wounded by a stomach shot and Lt Anderson did not return from a reconnaissance tour. In addition Vfw Wietfeld was killed and in the afternoon Lt dR Lichtenfeld, the company commander, was seriously wounded. Vfw Oesterlitz then took over command of the company.

Hauptmann Huber's Attack with I/72

Hauptmann Huber's I Bn was initially left in reserve, a decision which was to cost them dearly. Their history states:

To be held back in reserve might at first appear to be a most desirable proposition for a battalion, especially in the face of the adverse circumstances of the regiment's first Somme action. However, experience proved the opposite to be the case, as the reserve troop was often forced into an even more serious position, more often than not within the ranks of some completely strange troop section, and not with regimental comrades.

This was the doubtful fate of I Bn, which at first had to seek shelter in the cellars of Flers on 15 July, at the disposal of the regiment. During the course of the morning it was placed under command of Oberstlt Grautoff, IR 26, and received the following orders: "The northern part of Delville Wood is to be cleared of the enemy!"

Infantry Regiment 26, which had been in the battle for the past 24 hours, held a position in the northern part of Longueval and along the great cutting from the church to the east (Princes St). I Battalion's orders were to clear the northern part of Delville Wood and to advance to the southern perimeter and retake the old German line up to the Sugar Factory if possible. I Bn was followed on the left wing by sections of III/153, providing flanking cover and communication with neighbouring troops.

Hauptmann Huber scouted the field of assault and went to see Hptm Rausch in the command post of II/26, on the road between Flers and Longueval, for further information. Regretfully the information that the wood was only held by weak enemy troops proved later to have been a serious error. An error which Hptm Rausch would later pay for with his life.

Entrenched Tommies with Vickers guns. (Ditsong National Museum of Military History)

I Bn (IR 72) then received the following orders from its commander:

1. Enemy patrols with machine-guns have reached the northern edge of Delville Wood.

2. The northern part of Longueval and the great cutting in the wood are in the hands of IR 26 and companies from other regiments. Regiment 107 is to attack the eastern perimeter.

3. I/72 is to seize the northern perimeter of Delville Wood, advance on the great cutting and then to the southern edge of the wood.

4. The 3rd and 4th Companies are to advance on the road from Flers to Longueval as far as the large depression 300 m north of the wood and from that point prepare to advance on the wood. The advance must only be started when sharpshooters from I/72 and II/72 are visible on the heights to the left rear.

5. I and II/72 and Machine-Gun sharpshooter Troop 70 under Lt Richer are to advance to the high point along the road from Flers to Ginchy.

6. Machine-Gun sharpshooter Troop 70 will make available one machine-gun each from the 3rd and 4th Companies. The remainder under Lt Richter is to advance to the high point along the Flers-Ginchy road to the command post of I/72.

The companies deployed in admirable order under flanking cover from II/153. The entire area of attack lay, however, under heavy enemy high-explosive and shrapnel bombardment, intensified by infantry and machine-gun fire at the appearance of the 3rd and 4th Companies. As a result their losses were very heavy.

As soon as troops pressed forward to the edge of the depression, massive machine-gun fire was concentrated on them. The 3rd Company commander, Lt Schenk, jumped up and called to his men: "Company follow me!" He was killed instantly. A youthful hero with excellent military talents had paid dearly for his high ideals.

Lt dR Paschke and Lt Tetzner were wounded and Lt Ott took command. The 4th Company was in similar straits. Lt dR Krieger was killed at the start, closely followed by the company commander, Oblt dR Schoepke. Leutnant Ott from the 3rd Company then combined both the 3rd and 4th Companies under his command, as all other officers were either dead or wounded.

The 1st and 2nd Companies experienced the same difficulties. The approaches to the wood were under such heavy enemy bombardment that any further advance was impossible. These two companies soon lost all of their officers and the assault broke down.

Some courageous men nevertheless attempted to reach the objective, but were killed or wounded. The remnants of the companies dug in about 150 m from the perimeter of the wood. The 9th Company of III/153, which was placed at the disposal of I Bn at short notice, advanced into this position to strengthen the line. Their own artillery supporting fire was very disappointing.

This was one of the blackest days of I Bn. Only a small remnant with two officers was still operational. The rest, including all officers, were dead or wounded. The battalion had been ordered to advance against a heavily defended wood in broad daylight and in perfect view of the enemy, without any artillery support or preparation whatsoever, but in the face of an extremely heavy enemy artillery bombardment.

The assault was doomed to failure, just as the advance of RIR 107 on the same line at the same time was doomed. The same fate awaited IR 153 during its advance that night. Hauptmann Huber was furious that they had all been abandoned.

1.30pm: The German IR 72 (Thüringians) under Hauptman Huber attacked in the north-east but were driven off, losing almost all their officers.

3.00pm: The IR 6 Regiment of the 10th Bavarian Division attacked the eastern perimeter astride the Ginchy Road but were unsuccessful.

The Sugar Factory (Waterlot Farm)

The Sugar Factory – Waterlot Farm – pre 1914. (T Fairgrieves)

On 15 July the British launched an attack against the Sugar Factory. The Bavarian company positioned there sent out a plea for aid upon which a platoon of the RIR 106 was sent to their assistance. However, the British attack was so severe that all German troops withdrew out of the totally destroyed factory by evening. Their losses had been extremely heavy.

Planning the Midnight Attack

At 8.30pm the regimental commander (Oberst Kőnemann of the IR 153) was ordered to the brigade headquarters in Le Transloy and there given orders to attack Delville Wood with his regiment at 12 midnight, following heavy artillery preparations. II Bn was returned to the regiment for this purpose; also III Bn in so far as it was not in action already. However, neither battalion was available at the time.

Delay was requested but refused, as every second on the front was valuable. The meeting at brigade headquarters ended at 9.15pm. On returning to Gueudecourt, the regimental commander issued orders by word-of-mouth to I Bn and the Pioneer Company and in writing to II Bn. III Bn could not be found and did not receive any orders.

The plan was to attack Delville Wood at midnight; II Bn on the right wing over Hill 140, I Bn to the left, both with about 400 m area in which to deploy. The attack was to begin at the north-east and move to the south-west, into Longueval. To the left of IR 153, the attack would be supported by RIR 107 under command of Oberst Graf Wuthenau. Artillery preparation would continue until midnight.

The Prussian IR 72 were to support the attack. The remnants of I/72 (Hptm Huber's Bn) were to advance on Longueval and attempt to clear the northern part of the wood from there. This order would have been given to Lt Poppe, but the messenger, Lt dR Dorst, acting adjutant of I/72, was wounded en route.

Only the remnants of the 3rd and 4th Companies were informed and were able to advance to Longueval under Utffz Mattersteig, where they joined the 7th Company under Lt dR Backhausen. The remnants of the 1st and 2nd Company were ordered back to Flers during the night. Lt Krueger was given command of the combined companies and placed under orders of II Bn.

Summary of Events – Saturday 15 July 1916

12.35am: The IR 72 of the 8th ID left the Bapaume area to march to Delville Wood.

6.00am: The 2nd, 3rd and 4th SAI enter Delville Wood at the south-east corner under Lieut-Col William Tanner.

8.00am: The wood south of Princes Street was occupied by 3rd SAI.

9.00am: The 2nd SAI gain the northern perimeter.

9.00am: II/72 reach Longueval. The 8th Coy under Lt Penzler reaches Hill 140. III/153 is placed under Oberstlt Grautoff of the IR 26.

11.30am: The 3rd SAI (B and D Coys) attack German positions east of the wood killing 32 men and capturing 72.

12.30pm: II and III Bns of RIR 107 attack in the north-east but are beaten off.

1.30pm: The I/72 under Hptm Huber attack in the north-east and lose nearly all their officers.

3.00pm: The IR 6 of the 10th Bavarian Div attack unsuccessfully in the east.

4.30pm: The unsuccessful German attack from the Flers Road area.

6.00pm: A second unsuccessful German attack from the Flers Road area. The German rate of shell fire increases after dusk. The 1st SAI sent into Delville Wood from Longueval.

8.30pm: Oberstlt Könemann of IR 153 is ordered to attack the wood at midnight.

6

Fighting escalates – Sunday 16 July

2.35am: General Lukin was ordered to attack the north-west side of the wood, in order to seal off the northern entrances to the village.

6.00am: The 4th Battalion B and C Companies [Transvaal Scottish under Major Hunt] returned from assisting the 26th Brigade.

Private Eddie Fitz (2nd Bn HQ) and his friend, Private Henry Oldfield, were both wounded, so assisted each other as best they could:

> In the early morning [16th] we went to a dressing station which I had noted was just outside the wood's perimeter. We got his arm in a sling to keep his shoulder up. As soon as we got into this dressing station a chap said, 'No. I can't look after you – get back down the road!'
>
> So we went down the road toward Bernafay Wood. When we got there they wouldn't look at either of us. They simply gave us an anti-tetanus injection, put an anti-tetanus label on us and said, 'Get the hell out of it'. When we came out of the wood in the morning you could hear the 'dickie' birds calling, it was so quiet.

Padre Eustace Hill made himself as useful as he could:

> After spending the night in Bernafay Wood dressing station cooking Oxo, I left my servant Waigel and walked into Longueval through a mass of fallen houses. I found Capt Miller, 1st SAI Battalion. I sat in his trench for a bit, then left him and found a dressing station in a half ruined house, where Dr Bates, of the Black Watch, was MO [Medical Officer].
>
> Cooked Oxo in the yard until a shell brought the roof onto my pot and a brick on to my helmet, and another fired a house near us, which set two other houses on fire, causing them to blow up. I reported the fire to Capt Miller, and said the well should be cleared of wood and its iron cover put on to prevent its being filled by debris, and recommended all to fill water bottles.

North-west corner. (*The War Illustrated* Vol VI)

10.00am The 11th Royal Scots attacked northwards in Longueval while the 1st SAI Battalion A and B Companies attacked the German-held north-west corner of Delville Wood. They were supported by Major Hunt's 4th Battalion A and D Companies.

Captain George Miller, 35, (1st Bn B Coy) was a Londoner who had served in the South African War, then fought in the Kimberley Regiment at Trekkopjes. He was their 2IC in France (C Company) until transferred to the Eastern Province B Company. The platoon commanders were Lieutenants Leonard Isaacs, Arthur Craig and Fred English.

The 1st Battalion A and B Companies under Captains Jowett and Miller left their trenches and charged forward – into a hail of machine-gun bullets. Men were scythed down by the withering fire; Captain Miller being among the first to fall.

In B Company L/Cpl Joey Pattison was particularly concerned about his younger brother, Victor. He recalled Nash's abortive attack on the German redoubt:

> So when we got the order that the redoubt had to be taken with what was left of the men, we just looked at one another but Lieut Craig said, 'Get ready, we are going over in ten minutes time'. As soon as we were ready, in filed the platoon that was going to hold the trench while we were busy.
>
> Then I saw Lieut Craig pull out his revolver, give it a flourish over his head, and shout, "Come on boys" and over we went. Well, the next few minutes were hell let loose. I was knocked down two or three times by bombs bursting round

me, and in front of me. I could see dozens of arms coming up over a trench and flinging bombs.

Then I saw the few lads still on their feet retiring, and I went with them and found myself one of the lucky ten that had got back unwounded, while two others [Faulds and Estment] arrived bearing our lieutenant, badly wounded in six places.

At once I asked for Vic who, in spite of a shrapnel wound in the leg, was with No 1 Section on the right, and found that he had been left on the edge of the German parapet with a bullet in the forehead …

He later wrote to his parents of Vic's death:

On the morning of that awful day, the 16th, I took him his rations, and he couldn't have been in better spirits considering that we had then been fighting for twelve days.

Well, about midday [sic 10.00am] we got the order that a bombing trench held by the enemy had to be taken, so we assembled and went over the top. I being with No 4 section on the left, and Vic with No 1 section on the right.

We found that trench so strongly held that we had to retreat. When back at the lines I asked for Vic and his chum told me that he and Vic in charging with the rest had got right up to the enemy trench, where they found things so hot that they got into a shell hole, and started throwing their bombs into the trench ahead. 'B' [Pte Basil Wallace?] says he then looked round and found he and Vic were about the last left, so he called, 'Come on, Vic' and got no answer.

Victor had answered that greater call, mother, and could speak to us no more. 'B' bravely ascertained that Vic was quite gone before he bolted back for his life.

We made a great effort to get their bodies, but it was impossible, so Vic lies with the other lads on the German parapet. All the fellows are full of praise at the pluck Vic showed, and though I am absolutely sick about it, it comforts me to think he died like a hero. Don't fret about me, I've had wonderful escapes, was once buried by shell but am quite unharmed …

Private William 'Mannie' Faulds, 21, (1st Bn B Coy) from Cradock acted as a runner for Lieut Arthur Craig of East London. The latter lay wounded 75 yards from a German machine-gun:

I got hit twice in the left shoulder. It seemed that I hadn't an earthly hope. Then Faulds in broad daylight – it was about 10.30am – climbed the barricade and crawled to me. He was accompanied by Private [George] Baker and another man [Pte Alexander Estment].

It took them 25 minutes to drag me over the barricade. They pulled me by the left leg. One of my rescuers [Baker] was badly hit (two serious wounds) and it was a miracle that any of us got out alive.

Pte Mannie Faulds rescuing Lieut Arthur Craig.
(Painting by W Bagdapopulos in the author's collection)

> I was particularly impressed by the masterly way Faulds, the leading spirit, handled the situation. While lying on the ground my tunic was torn to shreds by machine-gun bullets, my equipment cut to pieces and my water bottle splintered to pieces.

Meanwhile Lieut Isaacs was sheltering behind a slight rise in the ground with five men from other companies. He asked Pte Emile Mathis, 17, to request reinforcements from HQ and tell them that he would try to get back under cover of darkness that night.

Sherman took part in the bayonet charge, but was luckily knocked back into the trench by a man who was hit. He crawled forward past the wounded, then saw a German officer and managed to down him with his second shot. He returned for his kit and while buckling it on was shot in the shoulder by a sniper.

Private Jack Atterbury, 18, was impressed by Faulds' bravery, thought that Lieut English bore a charmed life and recalled that Lieut Isaacs was "a hell of a nice guy".

Private George Miller from Miller Station near Aberdeen had attended Grey College in Port Elizabeth. He wrote that Norman and Cecil Featherstone had been wounded and Jim Foxcroft killed.

Sergeant John 'Charlie' Hurlin, 23, was 5 ft 4 inches tall. He was shot below the right knee and fell into a shell hole. A bullet hit his helmet, then a friend was killed and fell on top of him. Hurlin managed to hobble 50 yards to a dressing station while being sniped at.

Also in B Company, Sec-Lieut Fred English led a bombing party, one of whom, Pte F Dromgoole, was wounded. Their endeavours enabled the 1st Battalion to escape the attention of snipers for some time.

Gordon Smith and Richard Carter had charged forward together. Gordon later wrote to his sister, Ann:

> On Saturday night the Huns made a very heavy attack but they were beaten back. On Sunday morning at 9 30[am] we got the order to prepare to charge. At 10.00am we climbed over the parapet & charged with the bayonet. Although we had to go thro heavy rifle fire we reached our objective. Dick Carter was killed while climbing over the parapet into a piece of Hun trench. He got a bullet thro' the head & another thro' his left shoulder.
>
> I myself was wounded in the right wrist & right thigh. Its hard luck losing Dick but I paid his debt. I shot two Huns & killed four others with hand grenades. That's good enough for him & I. I suppose poor Mrs. Carter is expecting me, as Dick's bosom pal, to write & tell her all about it. But I can't. I never had a harder job to do in my life. It's so hard to put what you really want to say, in this case, on paper.
>
> I wish you would go up to her & tell her how he was shot. You can tell her that I was with him right to the last. He was alongside me when he was hit. He never suffered any pain, he was killed instantly. Must have been. Because when I crawled over to him to see if he was dead or wounded about two minutes after he fell, he was dead already.
>
> It was thro' going back to him that I got hit. I couldn't leave the dear chap in the lurch if per chance he was only wounded. Before we went over the parapet he told me if I come out alive & he did not, I was to send his love to all at home & especially his mother & dad.

According to Lieut-Col Croft the 11th Royal Scots had a torrid time in Longueval, on the left flank of the South Africans:

> It was very difficult to reconnoitre owing to the sniping: however we gave them a really good doing with Stokes [mortar] and that funny old trench mortar which looked like half a dumb bell, and then we attacked with one company, while another was ready to exploit as soon as the leading company gave them room to manoeuvre,
>
> South Africans were attacking on our right, more in Delville Wood; as a matter of fact we had to finish up at the bottom of the hill. And as we were already commanding that side of the village it was not a particularly necessary operation from our point of view.

We tried and tried all that day to cut through the impenetrable undergrowth stuffed with machine-guns, but our progress was slow and slight. The South Africans had no better fortune in the tangle, and late in the afternoon we gave up the attempt …

The 11th Royal Scots had wounded men left lying in front of the German positions. Lieutenant Turner and Sergeant Allwright went out to fetch them, just as Faulds, Baker and Estment had done for Lieut Craig. According to Croft:

[They] crept cautiously into the orchards and hoisting the wounded men on their backs crawled with them into safety. Gusts of bullets stirred the undergrowth as they performed this noble feat, but by rare good fortune neither the officer nor the sergeant were hit.

Remember these two had been on the rack for three days and three nights, and on top of that they had been fighting all day under close machine-gun fire which had killed several of their men. In all VC stunts the conditions are as important as the deed itself, and this deed was on all fours with many a pre-war VC.

Meanwhile C and D Companies of the 1st Battalion were placed under the orders of the OC of the 2nd Battalion (Major Harry Gee) for the defence of other portions of the wood. The Seaforth's Pioneer Company wired the east side of Delville Wood from Princes Street northwards, which took them until the night of the 17th.

(*Deeds that Thrill the Empire*)

The officers were particularly sought by German snipers, who were expertly camouflaged in hides, most of them in trees. As he had expected, Second-Lieutenant Allan Haarhof was shot and killed while organising his men's firing positions. Private Harold Ashworth recalled:

> Allan had only been in the firing line a couple of hours when a miserable sniper with his explosive bullet did for him … You remember how old Allan used to quote 'once more into the breach dear friends'.

Later he wrote nostalgically:

> We see a piano so seldom that I nearly weep with joy when I see one. Since I shall never again be able to hear those wonderful impromptu, half serious, half foolish efforts of Allan's upon any piano at any old time …

11.00am: The Cameron Highlanders captured Waterlot Farm (the Sugar Factory). General Lukin then visited the wood and was advised by Dawson that the men were exhausted.

2.30pm: Major Hunt's two companies (4th Bn B and C Companies) were relieved and withdrawn to the sunken road south of Longueval.
Lieut-Col Tanner was to write further of Lieut Walter Hill (2nd Bn B Coy):

> The following day [16th] Lieutenant Hill led a party of men to reinforce the line in Strand Street where he continued to display the greatest gallantry but was unfortunately killed (while leading a bombing party). Lieutenant Hill showed most conspicuous gallantry and devotion to duty throughout Delville Wood and by his actions there I consider earned the highest posthumous award [The Victoria Cross].

Private Bob Grimsdell (4th Bn) had been wounded in the neck and left for dead:

> I regained consciousness to find myself among assorted dead bodies including a German sergeant-major wearing a tasselled sword bayonet. His helmet with the gold eagle was in good condition except for the bullet hole in front.
>   I don't know how long I'd been lying there and in my dazed state I tied helmet and bayonet on to me. I then crawled away from shell hole to shell hole. A British soldier, one of the walking wounded, gave me a hand in finding a 1st Field Dressing Station.

Harry Cooper, 18, (3rd Bn C Coy) was a drummer and bugler from Johannesburg. As a boy scout he had won an award for bravery when he stopped a runaway horse in the city. Cooper was used as a regimental runner in the wood. His route from the south-east corner would generally have been to brigade HQ at Buchanan Street and back. He encountered many memorable events while he ran:

> One man was doing a one-man army job with a machine-gun placed on a mound of earth and cannon shells. Who was helping him I could not know or see. He looked towards where I was running and in a second I was facing the business end of his gun. His grin was a pleasure to see when he turned it Jerrywards again – and so was mine, perhaps.
>
> Looking toward the centre of the wood I heard one of the 'big ones' coming and hit the grass. The next thing I saw was that this 'chap' had skidded in some way, hit a large tree and stood upright on its base – a very big 'dud'.

Pte Harry Cooper.
(Springbok Sept 1972)

Later some wag placed a tiny shell alongside it and wrote 'The Long and the Short' with some kind of white powder. This lot had gone when I passed a day later. Something must have disliked the joke, only a big crater remained. Possibly it was delayed action. I could not say …

An unexploded British shell. (I Weisser)

Our padre [Rev Hill] came across my pal and I while we were trying to do something for the bad cases. He asked me if I would like to be 'OC Fires'. At first I thought he was joking, but he said to me, 'Come on, let's get a fire going and give some of the wounded something hot to drink, and to my pal he said, 'Get what Oxo cubes you can'. This is the middle of the wood and hell all around us.

Needless to say my pal and I pleaded guilty to sheer funk. He said, 'Yes, I can understand that, but we have got to do something'. I believe he found an old cellar farther back, but how far he got with the hot drinks I do not know. Later I saw him with both hands bandaged and still battling with the wounded. What a man – and if top decorations were to be given, he should have had 'Double Rations'.

Padre Hill continued assisting the wounded:

Capt/Padre E St C Hill.
(St John's High School)

Kept Oxo and tea going for wounded. An order came for us to evacuate, as the town was going to be shelled by our guns. I was asked to clear a cellar full of wounded men. I found the steps blocked by a man hit badly in the stomach, who refused to move or be moved. Below him was a captain hit in the arm and leg. I got him past and then got the rest up.

I asked them all to commit themselves to God's protection, and carried the captain, with other stretcher-bearers, to Bernafay Wood, through fairly heavy shell fire. All got through safely, despite mud and rain.

Returned to Longueval. Put a badly wounded patient in a bed I found in a house nearby, but that night we were ordered to clear out. Doctor Laurie, SAMC, helped me carry this bed-patient. Rain and mud awful. Some Highlanders helped us, and we finally got them to Bernafay Wood. I got to bed 5.00am.

That night Walter Giddy (2nd Bn D Coy) had to help mop up a German breakthrough:

We held the trench and on the night of the 16th July they made a hot attack on our left, 16 of them breaking through, and a bombing party was called to go and bomb them out (I was one of the men picked). We got four and the rest of them cleared out. It rained all night, and we were ankle deep in mud, rifles covered with mud, try as we would, to keep them clean.

German perspective

12.30am: The IR 153 (Altenburgers) attacked the northern perimeter. According to their records:

The time was about 12.30am before the first line finally reached the wood. About 50 m in front of the wood the troops were suddenly subjected to massive infantry and machine-gun fire and heavy losses were incurred, bringing the attack to a standstill. The troops had to dig in swiftly and try to launch a counter-attack.

On the outer right flank parts of the 6th and 8th Companies had penetrated the gap between the road and the wood (west of Hill 140). The II Bn commander, Major Von Stosch, his adjutant, Lt Haller, the 6th and 8th company commanders, Lts Greiser and Geitel, and about 80 to 90 men held this position.

As soon as the enemy fire had ebbed, patrols were able to establish that British [sic South African] infantry had apparently withdrawn into the wood and that only some machine-guns were stationed on the perimeters.

Major Von Stosch ordered that these machine-guns were to be taken from flank and rear, to open the way for his companies. At about 2.00am he moved into the wood with his men. He managed to gain about 200 m but in the darkness and heavy undergrowth of the wood he was unable to pinpoint the positions of the machine-guns. His company had heavy losses and as they day was dawning, he ordered the retreat and returned to the trenches in front of the wood.

The regimental headquarters learnt of these actions at about 3.30am when Major Von Stosch returned. He had ordered that only the minimum of men necessary to support the IR 9, 72 and 163 be left in front of the wood. About 80 men remained, mainly of the 7th Company under Lt Kurt Hoyer and a part of the 5th Company. The rest were recalled to Gueudecourt and re-organised into companies under Lt Berschmann and Lt Weidlich. The battalion was now commanded by Hauptmann Claassen, as Major Von Stosch had to return to the War Ministry.

On the left flank of the attack I Bn under Hauptmann Bieler had marched forward on the road Gueudecourt-Ginchy and then entrenched about 300 m off the edge of the wood in a natural trench parallel to the road. This battalion could also not keep to the specified timetable, and it was about 12.30am before I Bn could begin the attack.

This battalion also received such destructive fire from the wood that it had to withdraw into its trenches. Among those killed was the commander of the 3rd Company, Lt Hager. The enemy undertook a series of sorties, but was repulsed. The regimental headquarters received information on these actions at about 2 am.

Although the regiment did not succeed in its objectives, the attack did have the effect of keeping the British within Delville Wood and stopping their forward move. The short time given to the German troops and the resultant half hour delay until the attack, gave the British time to prepare their defences. They had also been warned by the preparatory artillery fire.

Gradually contact was re-established with III Bn, which was under the command of IR 26. Its 9th Company had supported I/72 in an unsuccessful

A group of German officer prisoners. (Ditsong National Museum of Military History)

attack on the wood and then entrenched itself in the front line of I/153. III Bn Headquarters and the other three companies lay under cover in and near Flers. The regimental headquarters and the regimental pioneer company lay in cellars in the southern part of Flers.

A soldier of I/153 recalled the assault:

We went into the trenches at 10.00pm. We had heard in the morning that the 72nd and 93rd Regiments and our III Battalion were to attack, and that the I and II Battalions, 153rd Regt, were to be in divisional reserve. We were sent into action in the evening, against Delville Wood. The assault was to take place at 12 o'clock.

We advanced to a distance of 100 yards from the wood. During our advance we came under artillery and machine-gun fire, so that we had to stop several times. In this advance our trusty company commander, Lieut Hager, fell. We dug ourselves in; as there were no trenches or communication trenches, every man burrowed a hole for himself.

Hauptmann Rausch's Dusk Assault

At 10.00am on 16 July, Hauptleute Bieler and Rausch, the latter of IR 26, arrived at the IR 153 regimental headquarters. Hauptmann Rausch had combined various parts of different regiments under his command and had entered the wood from Longueval. He suggested that a concentrated attack be launched on the wood from this side.

Rausch maintained that the wood was controlled by German forces up to and including the great east-west cutting. An attack supported by fresh troops of IR 153 would gain the remainder of this cutting and clear the northern side of the wood. However, these facts were in complete contrast to what Major Von Stosch of II/153 had reported.

The regimental headquarters agreed to Rausch's suggestion, as did the divisional and brigade headquarters when approached. Rausch was known as a reliable and excellent soldier. He obtained the following forces for his plan: 10th, 11th and 12th Companies and Pioneer Company, although the latter was not required.

The IR 163 (Holsteiners) III Bn came under heavy artillery fire at daybreak. They reported:

> Enemy air reconnaissance strong over our lines. At 4.00pm news of heavy fighting and losses of 9th Company came through. To find out more, an officer's patrol of the 11th Company was sent forward. They discovered that Delville Wood was heavily occupied by the enemy. The enemy advanced as far as the eastern edge of the wood but was pushed back by IR 153.
>
> After heavy fighting the 9th Company retreated some 400 metres, then, together with parts of IR 153, it occupied the north-western edge of the wood at around 10.45pm. The 9th Company remained with IR 153 for the time being. The remainder of the company together with the 10th Company were re-formed under Oberleutnant Westmann.

The Prussians of IR 72 were surprised to discover who their opponents were.

> Information obtained from prisoners told us that Delville Wood was held by a South African brigade with four battalions and supported by many machine-guns. Only two days later, after heavy artillery reinforcements had been brought in from Verdun and after Delville Wood had been so bombarded with heavy calibre weapons that the lofty oak wood had been reduced to firewood, did IR 153 succeed in penetrating the wreckage for a short time.

The IR72's III Bn fought in the north of Longueval and north-west of Delville Wood. It reported:

During the night of 15 to 16 July, and during the day of 16 July, six enemy infantry assaults were successfully repulsed by the 6th and 7th Companies, who had been supported by remnants of the 3rd and 4th Companies and by IR 153.

Musk Richter of the 7th Company managed to capture an enemy machine-gun during the fray. Richter had seen how the English had attempted to crawl forward with the machine-gun. Quickly he jumped from shell hole to hole and shot two of the three machine-gunners at close range. The third gunner was wounded by Richter but managed to fire his gun, though without effect, before Richter took him captive.

Again and again the English [South Africans] called to our people: "Hands up!" Quite without success, naturally. The enemy storm troops, some of them youngsters of 18 to 20 years of age, fell in the face of our fire within 20 metres of our trenches. Our men were standing upright, firing into the jumbled undergrowth, ignoring losses to their right and left.

The prisoners taken by our troops belonged mainly to South African regiments. Early in the day it began to rain, a most uncomfortable condition due to the loamy ground. In addition, the entire area between Longueval and Flers was under continual enemy bombardment so that communication with the rear was most difficult. Runners could only return by crawling, and needed half a day to return to the troops.

A wounded German soldier.
(Ditsong National Museum of
Military History)

Soon ammunition and provisions began running low, but fortunately some of our men found 300 hand grenades, 50 large shovels, and a sufficient supply of bully beef and mineral water in a hidden dugout. Ammunition and provisions were also taken from fallen comrades and enemies.

The 6th Company had been reduced to 23 men. With a courageous sense of duty the company had remained at its post, regardless of its heavy losses. The following were exceptionally brave: Utffz Gallus, Hauske, Evers, Smykalla, Reuscher and Vfw Schultz.

Remnants of the IR 72 company were withdrawn on 16 July in the evening. They were put to use bringing up ammunition and provisions to the front line until the 20th, when they were once more sent into action.

They found that 'Fighting slackened noticeably towards the evening of the 16th and during the night, most probably due to the deterioration of the weather.'

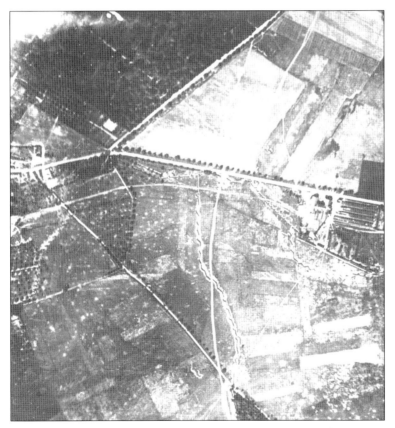

South Delville Wood, north Trônes Wood, Waterlot Farm and trench systems on 2 July 1916. (Mrs M van der Westhuizen)

9.00pm The IR 153 (Altenburgers) attacked in the north and were driven off. They were led by Hauptmann Rausch of the IR 26, who had planned the attack based on incorrect intelligence.

The attack was launched during the late afternoon and early evening of 16 July. It was a complete disaster. Hauptman Rausch was killed about 10.00pm, without realizing that he had made a grave error. The situation in the wood was not in the least as he had supposed. The great cutting was in fact only a lesser cutting close to the village.

The 12th Company had extremely heavy losses. Command over all troops fighting in Longueval and in the adjoining wood was given to Lt Stephan of IR 153 who reorganized the fighting sections.

This disaster and the reason for it became known the following day. An attack by I Bn for 11.00pm also came up against extreme resistance, since the Rausch attack had been unsuccessful.

The action was briefly referred to by Rausch's regiment, the IR 26:

> Attempts by II Bn, supported by additional troops of other sections, to eject the British machine-gun nest in the northern part of the wood were unsuccessful. Hauptmann Rausch was among those killed.

11.00pm The IR 153 repeated their attack and were again repulsed. The British withdrew to allow a bombardment of the village and north-west side of the wood.

The RIR 107 in the East

On the eastern side of Delville Wood the German trenches were waterlogged and exposed:

> On 16 and 17 July the RIR 107 suffered heavy losses in its unfavourable positions, which were flooded by mud from the rains. Leutnants Grimmer and Gebhardt of I Bn were killed on 16 July.
>
> The dead were, as far as possible under the heavy fire, buried directly behind the (front-line) positions. In addition, despite the sacrifices and activities of the doctors and their personnel, the evacuation and medical care of the many wounded was only partially successful.'
>
> The I/107 remained in its position in the Guillemont section, in a reserve position, and was to follow the fortunes of its other two battalions from afar, giving artillery cover when needed. The 4th Company helped repulse an attack on the Sugar Factory.
>
> On the 16th the 2nd and 3rd Companies were able to repulse an enemy attack being prepared at the entrance to Longueval by long-range artillery fire. It was observed that the enemy had heavy losses and that many wounded were carried from the area, with many subsequent burials. The I/107 continued to remain in its position.

The Third Line (Foureaux Riegel)

The Reserve Infantry Regiment 99 from Strassburg and Zabern in the Alsace was placed in the 3rd Line, which stretched from Ginchy to Foureaux Wood and lay between Longueval and Flers.

Heavy thunderstorms and cloudbursts discharged their burden over the bloody battlefield. The days alternated with scorching heat and cold nights, shivering the very marrow of the front-line fighters. Paths and trenches sank into chalky mire, the woods steamed and night mists flitted in ghostly forms across the bruised and mutilated landscape.

The regiment was placed under the command of the 3rd Guards ID on the 14th. The regimental staff, together with I, II and III Bns, was ordered into the Third Line south and south-west of Flers. The positions they were ordered to hold were in the process of being built. The trenches were only about 1,5 m deep and no dugouts were available. Work on the trenches began immediately and every soldier dug for his life.

On the afternoon of the 15th the edges of Flers were pounded with heavy artillery, particularly on the sunken road to Eaucourt and the sector held by the 4th Coy I Bn. On 16 July the bombardment of Flers became heavier. The left wing of the 5th Coy and sections of the 6th Coy came under very heavy fire from Delville Wood, from which they could be seen. Losses were heavy, so this dangerous 200 m section was cleared of troops.

Work on the trenches continued, but heavy rains during the afternoon and night made the trenches all but impassable and soaked the men to the skin. After dark an enemy aircraft circled over the positions and over the edges of Flers and fired off light signals. This was soon followed by a heavy bombardment. When the firing slackened work on the trenches continued. Work on dugouts was begun but came to a stop due to lack of shoring wood.

Summary of Events – Sunday 16 July 1916

12.30am: The IR 153 attack northern Delville Wood but are beaten off by infantry and machine-gun fire.

10.00am: The 11th Royal Scots (27th Bde) attacks northwards in Longueval and the 1st SAI (A & B Coys) in Delville Wood. Both assault forces are beaten off. South Africa's Pte William Faulds earns the Victoria Cross Decoration. Waterlot Farm (Sugar factory) is captured by the Scots. Gen Lukin visits the South African Bn Commanders.

9.00pm: Hptm Rausch of IR 26 leads attack by IR 153 which fails.

10.00pm: Hptm Rausch is killed during the fighting.

11.00pm: The I/153 attack but come up against strong resistance. The British forces withdraw to allow a bombardment of Longueval during the night.

7

Holding on – Monday 17 July

2.00am: The 11th Royal Scots and the 6th King's Own Scottish Borderers, both of the 27th Brigade, together with the 1st SAI Battalion were ordered to launch another attack on the north-west corner.

The attack failed principally because the bombardment was only for an hour instead of two-and-a-half hours. It was pouring with rain and pitch dark. The advance during the atrocious conditions meant that often fighting was hand-to-hand. Some Germans were bypassed in the darkness and they attacked from the rear. Captain Whitley of A Company [Royal Scots] was among those killed and his body was brought back to headquarters for burial.

5.00am: The attack by the Scots on northern Longueval and the Cape's A and B Coy men on the north-west corner of the wood had failed again.

Lance/Corporal Willie Catton, 39 (1st Bn A Coy), had served in the Uitenhage Town Guard during the South African war when in 1900 his brother, Gilbert, a corporal in Marshall's Horse, had been mortally wounded near Heidelberg, Transvaal. Willie Catton was hit and seriously wounded, but survived.

6.00am: Brigadier-General Lukin and his staff visited the wood. Lukin was based at the brigade headquarters in Montauban, however was often on the move trying to ensure that he had up to date information. Private Victor Casson of the Kimberley Company (1st Bn C Coy) climbed from his funk hole:

> I observed some distance away General Lukin accompanied by some of his staff peering through the fallen trees. Presumably they came to take note of the dispositions after the awful bombardment of the night before. I approached General Lukin and said to him, 'Sir, apparently I am the only one of my company alive; everybody I can see are either dead or wounded.'
>
> The general replied that I must remain at my position, as the brigade was about to be relieved. I retreated to my shell hole cover to wait for what was going to happen next …

(Deeds that Thrill the Empire)

General Lukin was accompanied by Lieut-Col Dawson, Capt Pepper and Lieut Sharpe, formerly of the Witwatersrand Rifles. He discussed the situation with Lieut-Cols Tanner and Thackeray. Tanner pointed out that they were thinly spread on the perimeters. Lukin later reported:

> I visited Delville Wood on the morning of the 17th and discussed the situation fully with Lieut-Colonels Tanner and Thackeray. Although I took the opportunity of again impressing upon these officers the necessity of digging in to the utmost, I was satisfied in my own mind that everything that could be done in that direction under the existing circumstances was being done.
>
> Officers and men were undoubtedly fully aware of the advantage to be obtained from digging-in, and they were only too eager to do so for their own sakes.
>
> I was impressed with the signs of strain and fatigue visible on the faces of officers and men, and fully appreciated what both Lieut-Colonels Tanner and Thackeray stated – that the strain and fatigue were seriously telling on their men.
>
> On my return to brigade headquarters I was told that you [Gen Furse] wished to speak to me on the telephone. On your doing so you informed me that the corps commander desired you to impress upon me the grave responsibility of holding Delville Wood at all costs. I replied that I fully realized this from the various orders which I had received.

At the same time, in justice to the brigade, I asked that the corps commander should be informed that I had just returned from Delville Wood and desired to draw his attention to the condition of the men, who were much exhausted after capturing the wood and with the strain of holding it for two days and two nights …

8.00am: Lieutenant Owen Thomas (3rd Bn A Coy) on the south-eastern perimeter reported to Thackeray that his company strength had been reduced to 71 and that:

My company has been so depleted, and the remaining few are now so exhausted, that I do not consider that we could put up an effective resistance if the enemy were to attack.

Private Norman Sturgeon crawled over to a wounded man to give him a drink of water, then was shot through the heart. He lay on the wounded man for 14 hours before being moved.

Private Frank Maskew (1st Bn M-G) and his Vickers gun team were kept busy:

That morning [Monday 17th] the Huns tried a counter-attack but we drove them back all right. All that day we busied ourselves digging in and the enemy maintained a pretty hefty shell fire at us. That night we experienced another counter-attack but the enemy was again driven back with, I think, pretty heavy casualties.

The Springboks repelling a counter-attack in Delville Wood. (*The Graphic*)

Padre Hill continued his ministrations:

> I walked to Longueval, Pte Waigel carrying my Oxo, etc. He left me and I
> started Oxo and coffee, a German bag of which I had found, and also I found
> sacks of tea and sugar and bacon and biscuits. Gave drinks to wounded while
> [Doctors] Liebson and Laurie dressed them. Returned to Maricourt 6.00pm. I
> left Maricourt with Cook and Waigel, 1st SAI. Buried Trotter by railway as we
> passed.

10.00am: Captain Sydney Style [1st Bn HQ] as acting adjutant requested mortar
support from Lieut Edward Phillips of the Light Trench Mortar Battery. Lieutenant
Isaacs had reported Germans digging themselves in 60 yards from his trench in the
north-west.

During the fighting a South African airman, Captain Allister Miller, flew over
Delville Wood and spotted for the artillery. According to Arthur Betteridge (4th Bn
C Coy):

> I must record an unusual episode which gave the infantry holding Longueval
> and trenches in Delville Wood a lot of encouragement. For several days a recon-
> naissance aircraft flew low over the German positions, pinpointing enemy gun
> positions for our artillery. He always appeared to be in the middle of archie shell
> bursts but carried on imperturbably.
>
>   This exhibition of bravery was also cheered by the troops in the trenches.
> Thanks to our fighter air patrols few German aircraft were seen from the front
> line. For that vital period of our advance control of the air was imperative. This
> particular Morane Parasol had a speed of only 80 miles an hour and the pilot for
> some reason or other was named by troops 'The Mad Major'. He seemed to bear
> a charmed life.

12.00pm: Lieutenant Frederick English (1st Bn B Coy) withdrew his men from a
position 40 yards from the Germans, to enable British artillery to shell it.

Sergeant Stan Griffiths (1st Bn B Coy) was joined at his Lewis Gun by his brother
Eric. When the latter was wounded Stan carried him to the battalion aid post – then
returned to the wood. By then B Company had dwindled to 46 men. Sergeant Hubert
Nicholson, 23, of Uitenhage was buried alive when his trench collapsed. He died of
wounds later in the day.

2.00pm: The German batteries at Ginchy began bombarding the wood. Private George
Garnet Tanner, 22, (2nd Bn D Coy) was employed as a company runner. Major Gee
sent him to Lieut-Col Tanner to explain what a serious position his company was in,
as most of his men had been killed or wounded.

He ran between shell blasts until he was blown into the air, turned a somersault
and came down into the shell hole head first. The sides collapsed on him, so he began

kicking his legs to attract attention. Fortunately "Other chaps lying nearby saw me and managed to extricate me".

Garnet Tanner delivered the message then returned to his company while under shell fire. He continued as a runner until he was wounded. He was later awarded the DCM for his bravery and perseverance in the wood.

4.30pm: A 4th Battalion patrol reported Germans east of Strand Street. Lieutenant Roseby of the Brigade HQ was sent to investigate and was mortally wounded. Meanwhile the 1st Battalion A Company was relieved by the KOSB (King's Own Scottish Borderers) and retired to Longueval.

7.00pm: As later told by the men of the South African Infantry wounded in Delville Wood … at No 4 General Hospital, London:

> The fighting was severe in Delville Wood and the South African Brigade seemed a small handful of men to tackle the job. Colonel W E C Tanner was in command.
>
> During the evening of 17 July as the Germans came in hordes over the top there was a distinct waver in the South African advance … Colonel Tanner then rushed forward, waving and urging them on, shouting, "We were told to hold this Wood at any cost and by God we will. Come on men."
>
> He was then seen to lurch forward and fall wounded in the thigh by shrapnel. He got up and again urged his men on until Delville Wood was ours. Every

Pte Garnet Tanner in 1914 after the train crash.
(A Tanner)

officer in Delville Wood was either killed or wounded in that advance [sic]. The colonel will surely get a VC.

Colonel Thackeray came up after the Wood was taken. He said, 'Good God, Tanner, you are bleeding to death.' Tanner was then carried off to a Clearing Station.

Lieut-Col Tanner was wounded in his thigh and was carried out, despite protesting that he wished to remain with his men. Lieutenant-Colonel Thackeray took overall command in the wood, while Major Gee took over as CO of the 2nd Battalion. One of the runners, Private Harry Cooper (3rd Bn C Coy), saw Lieut-Col Tanner being evacuated:

On another trip I saw men carrying an officer of one of the other regiments on an improvised stretcher. He was in a bad way and kept shouting, 'Take me back to my men'. But these men carried on oblivious to all the shelling and bullets … the colonel reached safety and lived to fight in many more battles.

Things were getting very bad now, wounded were not able to get much attention and water was hard to get. A pal of mine, also a runner, joined me in helping our regimental doctor do what he could for the wounded [The doctor was Captain Stephen Liebson, a Rhodes scholar and brother of the authoress, Sarah Gertrude Millin].

The doctor was only a young chap of Jewish extraction, and what a man! He appeared to fear nothing and worked like a Trojan dishing out tablets and bandaging with what he could get hold of. But he was facing a hopeless task.

I noticed that he was bleeding from the lobes of both ears, bits of shrapnel [splinters] were sticking into the lobes and told him so but he told me to forget it and keep on doing what we could for the bad cases.

There were not enough stretcher bearers to deal with the large number of badly wounded. Walking wounded were battling their way out alone …

German Events

2.00am: The IR 153 (Altenburgers) repeated their attack in the north but were again stopped by the men from Natal.

Parts of the Saxon RIR 104 and 107 became known as Regiment Wuthenau, named after their commander Oberst Graf von Wuthenau.

8.30pm: Oberst Von Wuthenau briefed his battalion commanders for assaults on the eastern side of the wood. Flers, the German garrisoned village to the north, was heavily shelled by the British. German troops advanced half-way into the wood up to Buchanan Street. A counter-attack then drove them back.

The Germans withdrew from the village and wood during the night in order to shell it. Guns had been brought from as far as Verdun to ensure that the positions be levelled by gunfire.

8

The Bombardment – Tuesday 18 July

3.45am: The British 76th Brigade and the South Africans linked up in the north-west corner of the wood. This did not last long, as the IR 72 (Thüringians) displayed dogged resistance in a rearguard action.

On the eastern perimeter Pte John Lawson (3rd Bn D Coy) recalled,

> It was as if night for ever refused to give way to day. A drizzling rain was falling in an atmosphere unstirred by a breath of wind. Smoke and gases clung to and polluted the air, making a canopy impervious to light. What a contrast was this Tuesday morning to the morning of the previous Saturday, when we first entered what was then a beautiful sylvan scene, but now everywhere a dreary waste!

Temporary Second-Lieutenant Clive Featherstone, 30, (1st Bn B Coy) came from Aberdeen, Cape. As a 15-year-old during the South African War his mother had sent him into the hills when she saw a Boer Commando approaching their farm 'Featherstonehaugh'. Despite her protests Cmdt Scheepers had her farm house razed, as her husband was in the field opposing them. Clive Featherstone attended Muir College then served as a lieutenant in the Graaff Reinet Commando. According to him:

> The day was fine, and we were not greeted with the usual morning counter-attacks of previous days. Major Macleod (4th Bn HQ) brought us instructions to take the last corner of the wood. This we did, but the orchard that abutted on it was smothered by machine-gun fire, and we formed our line along its fringe.
>
> An officer and a few men of another company came up to help us to hold the sector, but they were wiped out during the morning. Major Burges commanded D Company, on the left of the brigade, and he and I were the only officers left in it, although we had five for the attack on the 14th and had been reinforced by three more …

Our position at the head of the great salient we had pushed into the German lines meant that we came under fire from all sides, many shells coming obliquely from our rear.

At about 9.00am a heavy barrage came down and gradually increased in intensity throughout the morning, reaching its zenith at about 1.00pm. About this time a portion of the Camerons, on our left, were more or less annihilated, and our flank was in the air.

Private Frank Maskew (1st Bn M-G) and his Vickers team were part of the link up. He later wrote to his mother:

The next morning [Tuesday 18th] we got the order to go over the parapet. This we did, passing ever so many German corpses. We advanced about 500 yards to the edge of the wood and at once dug in. From here we could get a pretty good view of the Hun position and we could see many Huns walking about seemingly taking it easy.

We let them have a few bursts from our machine-gun and they scattered pretty quickly. This, however, was not a wise move, for though the shell fire was pretty bad at the time, yet it was not so much in our quarter. Now, however, the Huns must have detected the position from which machine-gun fire came and shell after shell burst most uncomfortably near us, and we knew we'd have to change our position.

Just as we were contemplating doing so, a shell exploded right on us and when the smoke cleared up three of our gun team were lying prostrate. One was my half-section and I went to him and lifted him up but on seeing the nature of his wound knew that his troubles were over.

The other two were seriously wounded but not mortally and, bandaging them as best we could, we got them taken down to the dressing station. There were only three left out of our team now. My poor old half-section, he was a good pal and I miss him very much and at night I often lie awake thinking of his mother who, like you, knows nothing of how her son met his end. I have written to her telling her all about it.

After this the shells came like rain and we were compelled to withdraw to our original position. Here the shells were not quite so bad and we felt a bit more comfortable. We stuck here about two

Pte Frank Maskew. (D McCarthy)

hours waiting for reinforcements in order to make an attack, but owing to the maintenance of a very heavy artillery barrage behind us, these were unable to come up and later on we were compelled to withdraw from the wood and occupy a trench just between the village and the wood [in Longueval near Buchanan Street].

Despite the link up in the north-west L/Cpl Joey Pattison (1st Bn B Coy) had had enough.

On the morning of the 18th news came that relief was at hand, but before the new division would take over, we had to clear the wood. I am certain if those in command had only known our reduced strength, they would never have given such an order when there was but a handful of us left. We had already made one attempt to take the redoubt on our left and had failed through want of men, and Jimmy Nash and others had fallen.

8.00am: The Germans unleashed a barrage from hundreds of guns, blasting the Springboks in the wood. At times the rate of fire would exceed 400 shells a minute, turning the wood into an inferno of explosions, flames and smoke which from a distance resembled a volcano. During the day approximately 20,000 shells landed in the wood, an area less than a square mile.

Private Gwyn Ashworth (1st Bn HQ) had been raised in an intensely musical environment, but he never became attuned to the music of the guns.

Talking of whizz bangs – one of these projectiles is not so bad but when you receive four at a time, representing an enemy battery, dropping in quick succession and in all sorts of unexpected places, you begin to understand what it means to say that there is a limit to human endurance.

It would be tolerable enough perhaps for one day, but when it is continued spasmodically for five days and nights with slight additions, such as shrapnel, high explosive (it makes a terrible roar on exploding and its fragments are dangerous for a range of 200 yards radius) 5.9 inch percussion and shrapnel shells, plentifully besprinkled, machine-gun, automatic rifle, the sniper pest at irregular intervals, and to cap it all – insignificant cover because you are too busy to dig yourself in, the state of affairs becomes more than merely 'lively', it becomes 'hellish' and one seems to be bordering on the verge of absolute lunacy and on the breaking point.

Such is the marvellous elasticity and adaptability of our nature, you hang on and eventually begin to flatter yourself that you have a fine disregard of all these terrors – until someone near you is hit and begins to moan in dreadful pain.

Then you have to begin again, laboriously piecing together the shattered fragments of your 'nerve'. It is not until you have been relieved and are on

comparatively safe ground that you actually appreciate how great the strain has
been and how absolutely glad you are to lie prone on the ground and forget …

Private Jack Carstens (1st Bn D Coy) believed the bombardment was the greatest
concentrated shell fire in modern warfare:

In the midst of this inferno our platoon sergeant approached me and said:
'Carstens, the Major [Burges] has told me to detail off one man to go forward
and silence that machine-gun. I detail you to go'.

It was then that, for the first time in my army career, I disobeyed an order. I
said: 'Sergeant, you can go to hell and do it yourself!'

'I'll report you and you will be shot,' he snapped back.

And I said: 'Sergeant, only a maniac would give an order like that and I refuse
to go. Get a dozen men and you lead us and then I'll go.'

The sergeant had no reply to that one. But he then detailed off Mackenzie to
go. I tried to prevent him; but Mac went and, before he had crawled five yards
into the open field he had a bullet through his side.

It was at this moment that the full fury was let loose. The shells came in their
thousands and we were trapped. My rifle and equipment lying next to the funk
hole were blown to pieces and my own escape from death is a mystery. I heard an
officer shout, 'Every man for himself. We must get out of here.'

Defenceless, I and the rest of our party began to move out of the wood. There
were hundreds of South Africans lying dead in that wood as I passed.

Mannie Faulds (1st Bn B Coy) again displayed heroism in going out under shell
fire to rescue a wounded man. For his continuous bravery he would be awarded the
Victoria Cross – the first South African VC of the Great War.

Charlie Ingram was lucky to survive. He recalled:

It was great fun potting German snipers who had been sniping from tree tops.
At times shells were falling at the rate of 400 per minute besides continuous
machine-gun and rifle fire plus tear- and chlorine-gas. It was estimated that
100,000 shells fell in the wood during the five nights and six days that we were
there.

2.30pm: The SA Light Trench Mortar Battery under Lieut Edward Phillips, 33, from
Queenstown, were sent forward from Montauban to reinforce those in the wood.
Phillips had previously served in the 3rd Battalion.

Padre Hill had little rest and later recalled:

Walked to Longueval. Intense bombardment of village and our trenches in
Delville Wood. Looted clothing for wounded with Stuart, 3rd SAI, and when
men's kit was gone I got women's clothes and baby mattresses, etc. I kept hot

(*The War Illustrated* Vol III)

drinks going until shell fire got too hot and my larder was badly hit and my equipment cut to bits.

I got all patients who could be moved down into the cellar and barricaded the door and both windows looking towards street, where snipers kept firing and shells bursting. Our house was hit at an angle twice. Burmester, Gordon, Sansom (of 3rd SAI) and two others couldn't be moved to the cellar, so I gave the three named the Holy Communion and put bags around the other three.

Now we saw the Camerons retiring and all who could hobble of ours left. Dr Liebson took a sergeant, and Dr Laurie remained. At last stretcher-bearers came and took all off. I helped carry Bailey (3rd SAI) to Bernafay Wood.

3.00pm: Lieutenant-Colonel Dawson was appointed CO and visited the HQ strong-point. Dawson placed 150 men in a trench south-east of Longueval.

Lieutenant Walter Hill (2nd Bn B Coy), who had escaped from the Germans on the 15th, was killed while leading a bombing party.

From 8.00am on Tuesday, the 18th, throughout the wood the South Africans crouched in their shallow trenches and foxholes, covering themselves with their steel helmets and arms, as the wood disintegrated around them. Shells reached a crescendo of seven per second, blasting the remaining trees and churning up the rich, dark earth.

(*Deeds that Thrill the Empire*)

The afternoon of Tuesday 18 July was to be the turning point in the battle as waves of fresh German troops awaited orders to attack.

According to a special correspondent the Springboks slogan was "If the South Africans do not gain their objective it will be because there are no South Africans left". Lance-Corporal H G H Kotze (1st Bn B Coy) wrote to his brother:

> Shall I ever forget how I jumped over the parapet with my pockets filled with ammunition, my bayonet fixed, and a few score yards away thousands of Germans advancing on us – when behold a deafening explosion took place, and was hurtled through space and landed prone on my back, to wake up finding myself confronted by a huge Prussian Guard.
>
> I gave the matter no consideration but quickly pulled the trigger of my rifle and he staggered back, shot through the head. Another came in his place, but he experienced the butt-end of my friend's rifle right between the eyes, and as he went down on his knees my pal rammed his bayonet through him.
>
> I had by this time regained my feet, and like Horatius, I tried to hold them at bay when another shell exploded, knocking me over and landing a hulking big German's body on top of me. There we lay for about 15 minutes, drenched in each other's blood, he dead and myself wounded, while several others walked over our bodies …

Second-Lieutenant Arthur Knibbs (2nd Bn D Coy) later wrote to his fiancée:

The third day the enemy started shelling us very heavily. I knew then that we were finished and that we could not get reinforcements. My captain [Capt Hoptroff] who was [later] killed rushed past and told us to retire to our headquarters trench.

I had gone fifty yards when I got it in the elbow just as I stumbled in a shell hole (lucky for me, might have got it in the head). I didn't feel much pain at the time I was hit, but I felt awfully weak on account of the loss of blood.

Ritches [Pte C H Riches] a traveller at Dreyfus and Coy (Ronnie will know him) helped me on from there to the advance dressing station. I should never have got through without his assistance. It was a terrible job, trees were cut down in front of us, and shells bursting all round.

Sec-Lieut Arthur Knibbs.
(Knibbs family)

At the dressing station it was worse, they bandaged me up and advised me to bolt for it. After having a bit of a rest I made a dash for it. Every fifty yards or so I rested. I shall never forget that run as long as I live. I saw men blown to pieces, and men lying wounded and killed all along the road.

When I arrived at the dressing [station] I collapsed, cried like a baby. They put me on a stretcher there, and [I] have been in bed ever since.

Second-Lieutenant Errol Tatham (2nd Bn HQ) made his way to the northern perimeter where he found Major Burges. On asking what he could do, he was sent to fetch reinforcements. Tatham collected a few men and returned to find that Burges had been killed by a shell blast. He was then hit by a number of bullets. He stumbled back toward his HQ, but collapsed in a shell hole.

Clive Featherstone. (Mrs M Stuckey)

Private Bill Helfrich (1st Bn C Coy) was a stretcher-bearer who tried to assist him, but Tatham died shortly afterwards. The position was then overrun by the Germans and Helfrich feigned death. After it was dark he crawled out of the wood and was picked up by English soldiers.

Captain Percy John Jowett, 29, (1st Bn A Coy) came from the Isle of Wight. He was sheltering with Sec-Lieut Clive Featherstone (1st Bn B Coy) near Strand Street.

Featherstone recalled:

Reinforcements enter the devastated wood. (Dept of Foreign Affairs and Information)

Major Burges sent his orderly to call me to instruct me about a withdrawal. Captain Jowett of C [sic A] Company went with me. We found that Major Burges had been killed by another shell bursting over his head.

Captain Jowett went back for instructions while I remained in charge of both companies, Captain Jowett being the last officer left to C [sic A] Company. I watched him as he walked back through a world heaving with explosions and sprayed with shrapnel till he disappeared in the drifting smoke and dust for ever [he was listed as missing death assumed].

The wood no longer existed as such – splintered stumps marked the places where great trees had stood. A little later we withdrew to where Col Dawson had formed a shorter line.

4.00pm Lieutenant Edward Phillips, commander of the SA Light Trench Mortar Battery, brought his men into the wood to fight as infantry. Private Gordon Forbes (LTMB) recalled:

[Light] Trench Mortar Battery converted into a company of infantry and proceeded to a wood beyond Longueval to assist SA Brigade. Advanced in extended order under heavy artillery fire …

Corporal Sam Sumner, 31, (4th Bn A Coy) had served in the Anglo-Boer War as a 15-year-old medic. As a Cape Town Highlander he was seconded to the LTMB from the SA Scottish.

> I learnt that courage, like cowardice, is contagious. Sick with fear, I crouched, bent double, behind inadequate cover. I was terrified and incapable of thought or action.
>
> An apparently unconcerned friend noticed my condition. 'Sammy, surely you're not going to let those buggers frighten you, now, are you?' Then my fears vanished. On occasion Padre Hill stood up fearlessly, amidst exploding shells and deadly bullets. 'Men, they may kill your bodies, but they cannot destroy your souls'. That was faith.

4.45pm The III/107 (Saxons under Von Wuthenau) attacked the 3rd Battalion D Company in the east but were beaten off. They were meant to secure the left flank of the IR 153, who were advancing through the wood. Enough of Captain Tomlinson's company had survived the bombardment to repulse them.

Lieutenant Francis Somerset's No 16 platoon was on the right flank of the 3rd Battalion's D Company. He was much admired for going to fetch supplies and post from the centre of the wood while under fire. Corporal Alfred Lilford, 35, recalled Somerset's wry sense of humour:

> He insisted on our shaving and tidying ourselves, saying that a corpse looked bad enough without our making ourselves look worse than we needed when our time came.

While trying to extricate his platoon later that afternoon Somerset was shot through the forehead and killed instantly.

Captain Richard Medlicott's 3rd Battalion B Company alongside also gave a good account of themselves.

Captain Wallace Frank Hoptroff, 43 (2nd Bn D Coy), from Bloemfontein had taken over from Major Gee, when the latter was killed, on the northern perimeter. He fought a rear-guard action until he found himself near the southern edge of the wood, where Private Frank Marillier, 20, [2nd Bn C Coy) described the 18th as absolute hell turned inside out:

> … Our lives were saved when a very brave officer, Captain Hoptroff made his way to our position. He wasted no time. 'Get out! Get out!' he said, and was almost immediately hit by a bullet and killed outright.
>
> It is strange how in the most urgent and tragic circumstances, one notices things of minor importance. For as Capt Hoptroff fell, I caught sight of his very beautiful gold wrist-watch; and have never ceased to regret that I did not take it

(*Deeds that Thrill the Empire*)

off and send it to his family ..." [Captain Hoptroff's remains were later found and interred in the Serre Rd Cemetery No 2, Beaumont Hamel, north of Albert].

A 6 ft 2 inch Afrikaner, Albert J Loubser, 33, had left his farm at Sir Lowry's Pass, Cape Town, wife and six children to become a stretcher-bearer. He later recalled:

Man, you know we were carrying with our stretchers backwards and forwards through that heavy shell fire in Delville Wood, and in the late afternoon we just had to sit down and rest awhile.

(*The War Illustrated* Vol VII)

An officer whom I did not know came up and said 'What's your name?' He wrote it down and went off. I said, 'Come on chaps, we're for it' and we carried all that night [17th] and in the morning [18th] another officer also took my name, so off we went again, but the shelling got so awful my mates said, 'No it is certain death to go into that wood'.

So I went in alone and carried men out on my back until I could carry no more! Soon after we were relieved I was told to report to the colonel and he said I had won the Distinguished Conduct Medal.

Arthur Betteridge (4th Bn C Coy), as a runner, was asked to take a cook named Geordie into the wood.

Entering the wood, just over the sunken road near Longueval, a particularly vicious salvo of shells exploded next to us. We ducked into a large shell hole and as I got up to go on, I felt as though a mule had kicked me and fell to the ground.

Pte Arthur Betteridge early in 1917. (A Betteridge)

I had been hit in the thigh by the nose cap of a 5.9 inch shell. I don't remember hearing the burst of the shell that hit me. A four inch hole appeared in my left thigh, breaking my leg.

As I sat up abruptly, I saw the nose cap next to me and tried to pick it up. It was still very hot and I dropped it. Geordie immediately pulled out my field dressing, carried inside my tunic; this bandage fitted nicely into the hole in my leg. I tried to stand up but found it impossible.

Geordie left me there and took the message into the wood. I learned later he delivered it to a corporal and returning from the wood was killed. We had both taken off our gas masks when I was hit.

I left my rifle and haversack in the nearby shell hole and crawled towards the sunken road. In spite of the shelling, gas and rain I fell asleep, completely exhausted. I cannot recollect any pain from the wound at that time.

On the southern perimeter the 2nd and 3rd Battalions' C Companies faced the wrong way. The 2nd had lost its last officer, so Sec-Lieut Garnet Green, 26, of B Company was detached to take command and lead the survivors back to the Buchanan Street HQ. He was ably assisted by a Boer War veteran, the Scottish Acting Company Sergeant-Major James McAuley Thomson, 35. The men filtered back using fire and movement drill against the massed German infantry.

The 3rd Battalion C Company alongside them were cut off. Acting Major John Jackson, formerly of the Queen's Bays and SA Mounted Police, heard that the Germans were approaching from the rear. He began organising a back-to-back resistance when hit and killed.

Second-Lieutenant Alfred Barton, 34, from Norfolk, took over and was last seen fighting hand-to-hand in the trench. Second-Lieutenant Harry Elliot, son of Lady Elliott of Benoni, was recorded as a prisoner, but was later accepted as killed.

The 3rd Battalion A Company managed to attach themselves to Captain Medlicott's B Company to their north.

On the southern perimeter Private Dudley Meredith, 20, (3rd Bn C Coy) and his companions cowered down in their trench during the bombardment:

The bombardment suddenly stopped at about 4.00pm. With a cry of 'There they come' we manned our parapet, but there was no sign of an attack from the Waterlot Farm side. After about fifteen minutes the barrage came down again with renewed violence and once again we crouched praying for the end, at the same time expecting and even hoping that that the next moment would be our last.

The bombardment suddenly stopped again at about six o'clock in the evening, and once again those of us who were still able prepared to beat off the attack. Again there was no sign of an attack from Waterlot Farm and we were wondering what was happening when there was a sudden cry – 'My God! Look behind!'

(*Deeds that Thrill the Empire*)

We looked back to see a line of Germans advancing through what under-brush remained and at once we knew that Delville Wood was again in German hands. Without thinking I jumped back into our trench and opened fire on the Germans I could see in front of me.

My mates thought that the better plan would be to retire back to the British lines diagonally across the fields in front of Waterlot Farm and without worrying about me away they went. After the war was over I learnt that although subjected to a very severe rifle and machine-gun fire most of them reached the British line unscathed.

A German appeared from behind a bush and instantaneously it seemed we fired at one another. His bullet hit our parapet about four inches from my left eye and shot some gravel into my face. When I cleared my eyes I saw him reeling and suddenly fall.

Looking round now I saw Lieut Barton on my left, lying kicking in his death agonies – how he came to be there I did not know. At the same moment I realized I was alone in the trench.

Another German became visible through the bushes and as I fired one of our men ran past in front of me. A second later, Sergeant Becker and two of our men, Lees and Hartz, came crawling into my trench, along with Scottie Ellis from the

Machine-Gun Corps, who was wounded in the back. 'Meredith, it's all up,' said Becker, 'and we had better try to get out.'

Accordingly we started crawling down the trench in the direction of British lines, but soon came to the end of the trench behind a clump of bushes. We stopped here for a moment to decide on our next move and no sooner had we done so than a German stepped round the bushes with his rifle trained on us. Turning quickly to get a shot at him, as I was at the end, I slipped and fell over in the mud at the bottom of the trench. The expected bullet did not come and on scrambling to my feet I saw Sergeant Becker and the others climb slowly out of the trench and put their hands up. I followed their example and our fighting days were over – we were prisoners …

Lieutenant-Colonel Dawson began withdrawing men from the shattered wood. Private Walter Giddy and his 2nd Battalion D Coy survivors were among them:

The Huns started shelling us, and it was just murder from then until 2 o'clock of the afternoon of the 18th, when we got the order to get out as best you can. I came out with Corporal Farrow, but how we managed it, goodness knows, men lying all over shattered to pieces, by shell fire, and the wood was raked by machine-gun and rifle fire.

Major MacLeod of the Scottish was splendid. I have never seen a pluckier man, he tried his level best to get as many out as possible. We fell back to the valley below, and formed up again. I came on to camp and was ordered by the doctor to remain here, having a slight attack of shell shock.

I believe the 9th took the wood again, and were immediately relieved, but the lads are turning up again in camp, the few lucky ones. If it was not for a hole in my steel helmet, and a bruise on the tip, I would think it was an awful night-mare … The lads stuck it well, but the wood was absolutely flattened, no human being could live in it.

Major McLeod was wounded, and I gave him a hand to get out, but he would have I was to push on, as I would be killed. Many a silent prayer did I send up, for strength to bring me through safely. I found a sergeant of the 1st all of a shake, suffering from shell shock, so I took his arm and managed to get him to the dressing station.

Just shaken hands with my old pal John Forbes. He is wounded in the arm and is off to Blighty. I quite envy him. A sad day for SA … They say we made a name for ourselves but at what a cost. All the 9th are resting on a hillside. Small parties of 25 to 40 men from the companies, which were 200 strong a short two weeks ago. We have taken back several miles.

Longueval

The evacuation of the wounded from Longueval to Bernafay Wood was a nightmare. According to Staff-Sergeant Welsh of the SA Medical Corps:

> The road from Longueval to Bernafay Wood was in an indescribable condition. It was impossible to carry from the front of the Regimental Aid Posts in Longueval, owing to the sniping, which was at times very severe and accurate.
>
> The rear was a mass of ruins, wire entanglements, garden fences, fallen and falling trees, together with every description of debris and shattered building material.
>
> It is one thing to clear a path along which reinforcements may be brought, but quite another to make a track on which four men may carry a stretcher with a modicum of comfort to the patient …
>
> Besides this road there was a narrow sunken lane, which at first afforded some safety, but later became so pitted with shell holes that the bearers were compelled to take to the open. In addition to these difficulties, it must be remembered that these roads were shelled heavily day and night.
>
> At times the enemy would put up a barrage with heavy stuff, which meant that no stretcher-bearing could be done until the fire was over. Parties who were unfortunate enough to be caught in one of these barrages spent moments of nerve-wracking suspense, crouching in shell holes or under banks, or wherever cover was available.
>
> One of the worst experiences of this kind was when it was decided to shell Longueval once more. Very short notice was given to clear all the Regimental Aid Posts, and only two men per stretcher could be spared. Padres, doctors, and odd men were pressed into service to enable all patients to be removed. As the party left, the bombardment began on both sides …

In order to bombard the German strong points in Longueval it was necessary to evacuate the British and South Africans in the area. According to the records of the Field Ambulance:

> On the 18th it was again decided to shell Longueval, in which Captain Lawrie had established a Regimental Aid Post. It was found to be quite impossible to move all the stretcher cases, so he decided to remain behind in his station.
>
> The Aid Post was in a building, and as the Germans were counter-attacking, and our troops going out, the windows and doors were barricaded with mattresses, furniture and anything that might stop a bullet. The bombardment was opened by both British and German guns, and for about nine hours a hurricane of shells was poured into the village …

(The War Illustrated Vol VI)

6.00pm: The Scottish 26th Brigade repulsed the Germans at the Longueval village square. According to Lance/Cpl Joey Pattison (1st Bn B Coy) the South Africans were involved in the fight:

> Well, what was left of B Company had to be relieved, as there were not enough of us now to hold the trench – a paltry 50 exhausted men left out of 250, all our officers gone except two sub-lieutenants.
>
> And the KOSB [King's Own Scottish Borderers] took over, and we went back into a reserve trench in the village and, half an hour afterwards, the trench we had held (and by so doing had lost our best pals – and I lost Vic) for five terrible days and nights was recaptured by the Germans.
>
> Well, all the Scots and South Africans who had been relieved were ordered forward again and a mixture of South Africans, Black Watch and Seaforths, dead weary from 16 days of fighting and five days of hell, charged forward again, cleared the whole wood and handed it over to the new division.

Private Frank Maskew (1st Bn M-G) and the remains of his Vickers crew also took part in the charge:

> After this the Huns came up and occupied the wood, at the same time the enemy artillery fire ceasing. The Huns, however, did not hold the wood for long, for with reinforcements we made a sweeping counter-attack and drove them far from the precincts of the wood.

The Germans are absolute cowards when it comes to hand-to-hand scrapping, but they are jolly good with their artillery, and their machine-gunners and snipers take a lot of beating. There were very heavy casualties on both sides and we have paid a great price for the possession of that wood, but the Huns, I think, must have suffered even heavier.

In that wood [village] a number of Scottish regiments fought with us and I never wish to fight with a braver or more cheerful lot. Most of them had been in the big campaign of 1915, but they said this absolutely put the tin hat on all their previous experiences.

That night when the survivors were relieved we were marched to a spot about two miles from the wood and there we rested.

In the Kimberley company (1st Bn C Coy) the Kirkman brothers had fared badly. Alfred, 25, was blown up by a direct hit of a shell, Doug, 23, was severely wounded and taken prisoner, suffering experiences which left him forever an embittered man, while Sidney, 20, was badly wounded and evacuated.

In the same company Dave Grindley had his legs smashed. He shouted for help, but his comrades had been told to get out and leave the wounded, who would be fetched later. He felt abandoned by his friends, however he was eventually picked up.

Staff-sergeant Welsh (SAMC) recalled the horrendous evacuation of wounded from Longueval to the Aid Post at Bernafay Wood:

Scrambling, pushing and slipping amid a tornado of shell fire, they headed for Bernafay Wood. It was impossible to keep together, and in the darkness squads easily became detached and lost touch.

The noise of bursting shells was incessant and deafening, while the continuous sing of the rifle and machine-gun bullets overhead tried the nerves of the hardiest. To crown all, it was raining, and the roads were almost impassable for stretcher work.

In fact, had it not been for the light of the German star shells, the thing could not have been worked at all. As the night wore on squad after squad of tired, soaked and mud-covered men stumbled into Bernafay Wood.

Here came a medical officer covered with grime and mud from top to toe, carrying a stretcher with a kilted Scot. Then a tall parson, unrecognizable under a coating of mud, with a stretcher bearer as partner, whose orders he obeyed implicitly. When word was passed round in the morning that all had returned alive, some were so incredulous that they started an inquiry pf their own.

10.00pm: Elements of the RJ13 [Reserve Jaeger] Saxons joined the RIR107 east of the wood.

11.00pm: Lieutenant-Colonel Dawson arrived at Thackeray's HQ and organised the evacuation of the wounded. In the wood Springbok survivors had clustered around

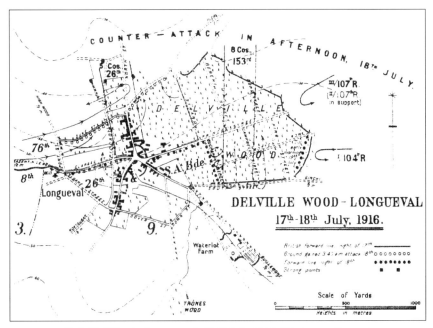

Delville Wood – Longueval 17-18 July 1916. (Ordnance Survey)

Thackeray's 3rd Battalion HQ in the south-west, the position originally held by B Company.

Dawson ordered Capt Sydney Style, 23, of King William's Town to evacuate the wounded. While carrying in an officer, Style was shot through the throat. Before leaving he wrote a bloodstained note to Dawson,

> I'm awfully sorry, sir, but it wasn't my fault; I'll get back as soon as I can.

11.59pm: The 26th Brigade relieved two companies of the SAI 1st Battalion and two companies of the 4th Battalion, who retired under Dawson's command.

The Regimental Aid Post and its occupants in Longueval survived the bombardment. According to the Field Ambulance records:

> … By nothing short of a miracle the Regimental Aid Post was practically the only place that did not get a direct hit. During the night, dressing the wounded was carried out under great difficulty, as only a small electric torch or candle could be used. Captain the Rev E Hill, who had also remained to help, managed to keep up a constant supply of tea and coffee, apparently from supernatural sources. On the morning of the 19th a counter-attack was driven well home, and Captain Lawrie's party was thus saved from capture.

German assaulting force

At 3.45am on the 18th July the British 76th Brigade and South Africans met up in the north-west corner of the wood. The Thüringian regimental history records:

> Two companies of the IR 72 acted as rear-guard during the early morning with-drawal. After the [night] bombardment of Delville Wood by our artillery, the 5th Company returned to its positions and the 8th Company received orders to once more hold its front-line position, whilst the other companies were being withdrawn.
>
> However, the enemy had noticed the withdrawal and had followed hard on our heels before the bombardment had started, so that two platoons of the combined 1st and 2nd companies under command of Krueger had to be sent to the Foureax Wedge in support.
>
> The 8th Company then found themselves in trouble. Under its commander Lt dR Penzler, the small band of courageous men managed to stop the waves of enemy advancing on their makeshift strongpoint, thus saving the entire regi-mental line from being rolled up.

6.00am: The German RIR 104 attacked the southern perimeter, but failed to pene-trate the defences.
8.00am: … onwards the German artillerists unleashed a devastating bombardment of Delville Wood.

3.30pm: The German bombardment ceased. Eight assault companies of the IR 153 (Altenburgers), commanded by Hauptmann Bieler, then attacked and breached the northern defences. They were surprised when smoke-blackened youngsters rose from the mud and debris to challenge them, holding them up in Princes Street.

4.45pm: The Germans were unable to breach the Transvalers defences on the eastern perimeter. The German Official History records:

> III/107 carried their assault, which was bravely launched, to within 30 to 40 m from the wood. There the South Africans, who had not been demoralised by the German artillery fire, fired accurately at the attacking Saxons …
>
> It appeared impossible for them to advance any further into the wood. Those in the shell holes who were still able to fight first had to try to subdue their many aggressive opponents with rifle fire and hand grenades.

According to Leutnant dR Tscherning of the 10th Coy III/107 (Saxons):

> At 4.45pm the great moment was at hand. Our artillery fire moved away from the edge of the wood to its centre. The whistle blew! Up and over and into the

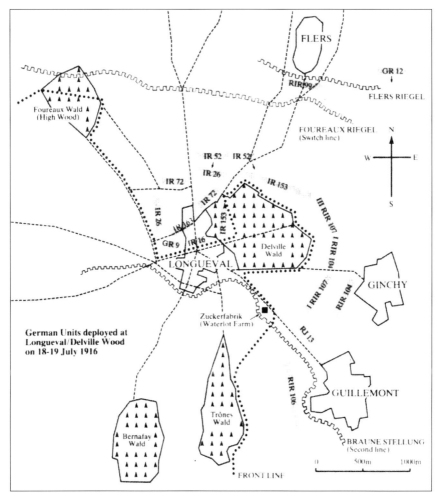

German units deployed at Delville Wood 18-19 July 1916.

wood! But suddenly we were greeted by heavy retaliatory fire from the wood. My men were falling left and right. I screamed out, 'Down! Down! Lie down!'

The British [sic South Africans] had sought shelter from the day-long bombardment in dugouts at the edge of the wood. These had previously been dug by German soldiers. They emerged to inflict such heavy losses on us that almost the entire III Battalion was destroyed.

There was nothing else to do but retire to our trenches in order to save what was left. That evening we moved further back to trenches at the Flers/Ginchy road.

The IR 26 storming Longueval. (IR 26 History)

5.00pm: The newly-arrived, fresh troops of the IR 52
Brandenburgers) advanced southwards through the wood and reached its perimeter
after overwhelming the defending troops there.

6.00pm: The IR 26 (Magdeburgers) and III/52 (Brandenburgers) then assaulted
Longueval, driving the 27th Brigade back.
    According to the Germans gaps were still found in their lines by the British.

> A more powerful English forward thrust advanced through the gaps that were
> still not closed, especially through the quite concealed road, lying just east of the
> village, and caused the mostly leaderless 153d great distress.
>   Well directed flanking fire caused numerous casualties, and especially effec-
> tive were South African snipers concealed in the trees. So the fighting against
> the enemy in the forest gradually went back and forth, connections were lost, the
> confusion became even greater, until finally darkness made an overview of the
> situation quite impossible.

The Germans began to fall back, with only the right wing holding the southern
edge of Delville Wood. Wounded officers made their way to the III/153 headquarters, where Major Schönberg at 6.50pm decided to take the IIId and part of the IId to
Ginchy. Their history continued:

It was a touching sight, this white-bearded man amongst his shot-up battalion! The old gentleman had crouched for the greater part of a day in a trench that was hardly knee deep and his battalion had torn forward over and over again up to the north-east edge of Delville Wood. How close this leader and his men came in the hardship and danger they underwent nobody can portray.

The order that he gave to the III Battalion at the commencement of the fighting will always live in the history of the III/153. 'We no longer have a flag here, my children, however, where my white beard flows, so stands the IIId Battalion.'

So thus it was during those difficult days … It deeply affected me when I brought the news to our Papa Schönberg that the regiment had been mentioned in the army report. The old man turned round and cried about his 'children' who fought here and had bled and had been killed.

Major Schönberg. (N Cave)

9

At all Costs – Wednesday 19 July

Eighteen men of the 2nd Battalion SAI, who had been captured by the Germans the previous afternoon, managed to escape during the night and joined Captain Medlicott's 3rd Battalion B Company on the eastern perimeter.

As Major Macleod had been badly wounded, Major Hunt became acting OC of the 4th SAI. He received an order timed 3.40am from Lieut-Col Dawson to retire to Talus Boise. He handed over to the Norfolk Regiment and extracted the remainder of his battalion from the wood.

When he reached Montauban he saw Gen Lukin, sitting on a tree stump, who asked:

> "You know, Thackeray is still in there, in the wood. Are you and your men ready to go in and get Thackeray out?"
>
> "Yes, Sir." replied Hunt.
>
> "What is your strength?"
>
> "C Coy 21; B Coy 19; and A Coy, lying down there, 6."
>
> "No!, said Lukin. "That would be no use. Stop where you are."

Charlie Stuart, 22, (2nd Bn C Coy) woke at dawn to find himself alone in his trench facing south. The survivors of his company may have made their way to Longueval or the Buchanan Street headquarters position north of them. German infantry had infiltrated the area and he thought that he was possibly the only survivor of the brigade.

He felt compelled to seek his comrades so, seeing a ruined summer house ahead, which would make an ideal shelter and observation post, he ran toward it. He saw a German drop to his knee and aim at him, so Stuart swung his rifle and fired wildly. The German dived for cover, enabling Stuart to reach the summer house and slide into a shell crater.

Private C B Stuart.
(R Stuart)

(*The War Illustrated* Vol VI)

After recovering he crawled to the lip of the crater from where he saw three German officers facing away from him. They peered through field glasses while discussing matters. Stuart decided that his contribution to the war effort would be the threesome, whom he duly dispatched.

Shortly afterwards a young German who was seeking cover jumped into Stuart's shell hole. They stared at each other then the young soldier began shouting that he wished to surrender. Stuart indicated that no harm would come to him if he would keep quiet. The youngster continued shouting for mercy so, in fear of discovery and reacting automatically, he shot him.

He never forgave himself for this. His training and self-preservation had kicked in and caused him to instinctively fire. Later he saw some Germans escorting South African prisoners, so raised his arms and stepped out to meet them.

At the Buchanan Street headquarters position Private Harry Cooper (3rd Bn C Coy) recalled how their colonel rallied them:

> During the night a voice kept calling out our war cry (I still do not know how to spell it) to keep us on the alert. It came from one of the finest gentlemen who ever breathed, our own Colonel Thackeray. He has since passed on, but his memory will never die while a 3rd Regiment is still alive …
>
> One day I was given a written order and told to do my best to get through to brigade headquarters. Off I went like a rabbit, through the village, down the

sunken road with all the 'devils of hell' going through me. You don't know how scared you can be until you are alone, entirely alone, surrounded by dead. Dead everywhere looking at you with sightless eyes and the smell made me feel bad.

Anyway I found my way and a non-com led me to the general's dug-out. I faced the general [Lukin], saluted, gave him compliments of our colonel and gave him the note. He looked at me with tears in his eyes and asked me to tell him something about his men in the wood. All the time he was exclaiming, 'My men, my poor men'.

I told him as much as I knew. He then told someone to get me a drink and a bite. Was I grateful for both. It appears that the note informed him that more stretcher-bearers were needed as regiments had been helping one another to carry out wounded.

My job was to show the bearers the way to the centre of the wood or to where they where they were most needed. I might tell you that I lost no time in getting along that road again, back to the wood. How the chaps following got on I don't know, but when we reached the wood and I found the colonel to report to, there were very few of them left. But the SA Medical Corps got right down to it …

8.00am: On the eastern perimeter the Germans overwhelmed the 3rd Battalion B and D Companies, who had run out of ammunition, and captured over 200 men. Captain Richard Medlicott (3rd Bn B Coy) later wrote to Col Thackeray:

(*Deeds that Thrill the Empire*)

Dawn 19th. Exhausted machine-gun ammunition. Drove off attack from wood but had to chuck it soon after 8.00am. No ammunition. Our men threw bombs, but we had only a few left. Many of our dead were exhumed by our heavy artillery, which hindered us at the wrong moment – at my trench east of wood. Damn those artillery garrison.

Handed back, sorry to say, all German prisoners captured during the day. I got not a wink of sleep for four nights. Could not sleep the night 18th. Got Lieuts Guard and Thomas in a safe place [both wounded] with German prisoners – irony. I was satisfied with our marksmanship, so many dead Germans round us in the wood …

Among the wounded was Pte Percy Land, who had been wounded at Halazin. Fortunately he did not wear a sniper insignia, as any found were shot out of hand.

Private Dick Unwin (3rd Bn B Coy) lay wounded in his trench when he saw a German officer walk over to a South African Machine-Gun officer and shoot him. Unwin tore off his sniper's badge with bloodstained fingers and pushed it into the mud. It was like destroying his death warrant. He was later led away with other walking wounded, his head swathed in bloody bandages.

When the Germans released their comrades who had been prisoners of the Transvalers they were surprised to find that they had been treated surprisingly well. Some pointed to luxuries which they had not seen for years, real coffee and chocolates. The attitude toward the South Africans changed drastically for the better.

Private Victor Wepener 19, (3rd Bn B Coy) was a descendant of the Boer hero, Louw Wepener, who was killed while leading an attack on the Basuto capital Thaba Bosiu in 1865. While Victor Wepener had acted as a runner in Lieut Guard's platoon two of his brothers had been wounded and evacuated:

Major V E Wepener DSO.
(History of the ILH)

> We were shelled from all sides. At times men were killed next to me while I was talking to them. Although I always had ammunition, the rain and mud got into our rifle bolts and caused them to jam.
>
> When the Germans eventually overran us, I was impressed by a very aristocratic officer who wore a cap instead of a steel helmet. He kept his hand over his pistol holster while we remnants were being collected in an open glade.
>
> A German soldier with a bandaged head and his rifle and bayonet slung over his shoulder called me 'Kamerad'. I didn't

quite know what to say, as I didn't fancy being his comrade. The German soldiers on average were jolly good chaps.

I then helped to carry Lieut Guard, who had been shot in the leg. He had been a manager of Stuttafords [clothing store] and had joined up as a private. Lieut [sic Capt] Pirie, who was 2IC to Captain Medlicott, was also taken prisoner.

Some of the wounded had to be left behind. I was one of the few to escape unscathed. We were then marched through their lines and we saw many Germans lying there waiting to attack.

A couple of our chaps carried a German with a stomach wound on a ground-sheet. Our artillery opened up and we were amused to see our guards ducking away and running for cover. After what we had been through, we didn't worry about shell bursts anymore.

Meanwhile, the remnants of the 1st Battalion B Company left the wood. According to L/Cpl Joey Pattison:

Well, next day [19th] we were given the order that all South Africans had to leave the firing line and return to our old starting point of the 14th, now far away behind the line and thither as I live – shells were still flying round as we dragged ourselves in two's and three's.

I shall never forget that day as long as I live – shells were still flying round as they had done the first day, and as I looked back at the wood, where nearly all my best pals lay, and my own brother, I was so weak that tears fell and Basil Wallace and I took one another's arms and helped each other out of it …

Private Frank Maskew (1st Bn M-G) recalled,

The next day more fellows who had lost their way rolled up, but what an apology we were for the fine brigade that set out. Everywhere could be seen fellows making anxious enquiries as regards the welfare of their friends.

It was terrible, that wood, and I don't think I shall ever forget it, but it was fine to see the way our fellows behaved and how well our officers carried out their duties. I am convinced South Africa will never have cause to be ashamed of us …

The Seaforth Pioneer Company dug a communication trench from the northern tip of Trônes Wood toward Pall Mall. This was perhaps for the evacuation of wounded or for bringing in fresh troops sometime!

Frank Marillier (2nd Bn C Coy) fought from the headquarters trench:

Holding enemy back in first line trench, but enemy snipers seem to be every-where. Poor Cecil Chilcott being among [the casualties] – shot through the eye. New division comes in and advances on the enemy right – but are repulsed.

Enemy counter-attacks four times but SAI boys are too good, though only a handful left. I am the only one left of my gun team. Only one 2nd Regt officer left, Lieut [Garnet] Green, and two of the 3rd Regiment, Col Thackeray and Lieut Phillips. This is the total of officers to the SA Brigade.

Padre Hill was fortunate to have survived the battle after five days of tending to the wounded:

Private L Frank Marillier. (Mrs M Marillier)

I returned [to Longueval] and found water short, so watched my opportunity and filled all cans, escaping snipers. [A German officer in a shell hole near the Longueval well shot men who crawled to it for water, but did not fire on Padre Hill, who disregarded shells and machine-gun fire while fetching water].

I brewed tea, etc, and later on about 30 stretcher-bearers came up, all of SAMC. Dr Lawrie and Welch came to the wood and returned with Capt Browne (4th SAI) and another. The Germans made an attack on the town, so I advised all unarmed stretcher-bearers to clear [off] with the stretchers. They did and I was left alone. I waited in our hospital for more wounded.

10.30pm: The 9th Division was relieved in the sector by the 3rd Division. Lieutenant-General Walter Congreve VC replaced the shattered 9th Division in the nick of time. He was born at Chatham, Kent, in 1862, educated at Harrow and joined the Rifle Brigade in 1885.

Congreve had won his Victoria Cross during the South African War at the Battle of Colenso, where he attempted to rescue Lieut Freddy Roberts, the only son of Lord Roberts, who was to be awarded the first posthumous VC.

Congreve married Celia la Touche in 1900 and had three sons. One of them, Major William (Billy) La Touche Congreve, 25, of the Rifle Brigade had already earned the DSO and MC. He acted as brigade major to the 76th Brigade of the 3rd Division during its relief of the South African Brigade.

Lieutenant-Colonel Thackeray and his band held out against all odds. They were constantly under attack. Thackeray fought like a common soldier, with rifle and bayonet, shouting the Springbok war cry and inspiring the men. On two occasions he crawled out of the strong-point to rescue wounded men.

According to Richard Cromwell [Militaria 7 (2) 1977]:

> The casualties inflicted on the Germans on the 19th, followed by Thackeray's successful defence of Buchanan Street that night were achievements which may well have saved the entire flank of the British front.

According to Sec-Lieut Edward Phillips, who fought alongside Lieut-Col Thackeray,

> On the night of 19 July, when the enemy massed and assaulted our lines, Lieut-Col Thackeray jumped onto the parados and threw hand grenades, and when enemy's grenades exploded, throwing him into the trenches he immediately got up and continued throwing grenades until the enemy's attacks were repelled.
>
> In my opinion, had Lieut-Col Thackeray not shewn his total disregard of danger, our men would never have fought the way they did in Delville Wood. Even when the situation was at a most critical stage, Lieut-Col Thackeray issued orders to hold the line at all costs, and when the men were absolutely beat by fatigue, he went up and down the trenches encouraging the men …

German movements

3.30am: Two companies of the IR 52 (Brandenburgers) were placed under the IR 153 (Altenburgers) to attack the south-east corner.

(*The War Illustrated* Vol VII)

4.30am: The German history states:

> Oberstlt Könemann, together with Lt Böhme, took command of both companies. They moved in columns on the route from Flers to Longueval, then over the northern corner of the wood along the large ride which splits the wood from north to south [Strand Street] through the enemy barrage without losses until they reached the large cross-ride [Princes Street]. Here they prepared themselves for the attack. The well-informed force of 220 men set off from the centre of the wood, one-and-a-half metres apart, and ran southwards until the front group reached the southern perimeter.
>
> Then the whole line swung to the left and the loose line of 300 m length moved eastwards in the direction of the rising sun. It was precisely 6.00am. The right flank had already moved in next to the forward posts in the wood, advancing in the light shrubbery.
>
> Only when the enemy noticed them at the last minute and opened fire, did the companies charge forward and overwhelm them. Five officers and 185 men of the 3rd South African Battalion were captured, together with three machine-guns.
>
> Over and above this, thanks to the clever actions of Lts Kuntzen and Martin, 16 men of Group IR 52, who were mainly unhurt, and the badly wounded Lt Zetzsche were freed and a German machine-gun recaptured.
>
> During this brave attack Lts Schultz, commander of I/52 [Saxons], Weber and Kniekamp were wounded, with the result that both companies had to fight virtually leaderless in the dense wood. Delville Wood was now finally again completely [sic] in German hands. It nevertheless cost a lot of the best blood to recapture it.

7.00am: The British 53rd Battalion reinforced Longueval.
  Oberstleutnant Grautoff of IR 26 (Magdeburgers) commented:

> … The English outmatched us both as far as strength of forces went as well as in being equipped with sufficient light machine-guns [Lewis-guns] and trench mortars. This type of weaponry was only issued to our forces at a later stage, following the experiences on the Somme. In addition, our own artillery fire which bombarded the south of Longueval constantly made this position untenable for us …

8.00am: In the east after the IR 153 Altenburgers and IR 52 Brandenburgers captured the Transvalers from the rear the Altenburgers were filled with admiration for the 3rd SAI:

> The prisoners were South Africans, partly of British, partly of Dutch ancestry. All of them very good-looking men. Some of them carried the badly wounded Lt Zetzsche and other wounded on improvised stretchers.

German officer POWs alongside blasted concrete bunker being guarded by a Jock.
(Ditsong National Museum of Military History)

Our wounded had been treated splendidly during their short period of captivity. Medical care, food and drink and cigarettes were offered in quantity and in a friendly manner. In addition, articles which had been unattainable luxuries for the poor Germans, such as mineral water, champagne, spirits, chocolates, ham, biscuits, etc, were handed around.

Once more confirmation was obtained that the British were in general decent opponents, against whom, incongruously, it was a pleasure to make war! The French were vastly different, for they showed extreme animosity on every occasion, sentiments which were mutual.

12.00pm: Two companies of the IR 52 (Brandenburgers) left Flers and advanced on Delville Wood.

4.00pm: The 4th Company of RJ 13 supported the IR153 in eastern Delville Wood.

10.30pm: The German II/GR 12 Regiment advanced to Princes Street.

Thursday 20 July

3.00am: The British attacked Longueval but were repulsed by the IR 72 (Thüringians). Second-Lieutenant Edward Phillips later reported on Lieut-Col Thackeray,

> On the second attack early on the morning of 20 July, he grabbed a rifle and fought with the utmost gallantry, by his acts inspiring the men to do their utmost.

8.00am: Lieutenant-Colonel Thackeray sent a message to Gen Lukin urgently requesting supplies of water and ammunition. Second-Lieutenant Garnet Green then advised Thackeray that the Royal Welch Fusiliers had entrenched themselves in the road running parallel to the position they held.

During the morning combined units of IR 52, IR 153, GR 12 and RIR 107 occupied eastern Delville Wood, but were unable to link up with Longueval. As a result Thackeray's HQ entrenchment was attacked throughout the day.

Private Frank Marillier (2nd Bn C Coy) took part in heavy hand-to-hand fighting. When the Royal Welsh Fusiliers retired he heard Thackeray shout at them to return to the line or he would shoot. Marillier added:

(*Deeds that Thrill the Empire*)

Heavy hand to hand fighting still continues. SA boys, tho' only a handful left, still hold enemy back. Royal Welsh Fusiliers retire – all for nothing. SA boys to the rescue. Colonel Thackeray splendid. Orders them to return and hold the line or he would shoot. We have been without rations and water for two and a half days, and no sleep for six days and nights …

Brigade-Major Billy Congreve DSO MC reconnoitred the enemy lines and drew up a plan of attack to relieve the South Africans. While writing his report near Longueval he was shot by a sniper and killed. Ironically he was awarded a posthumous Victoria Cross, making the Congreve's the second father/ son award of the VC.

1.00pm: Thackeray sent an urgent note to Lukin:

Major Billy Congreve.
(W Congreve: *Armageddon Road, a VC's diary 1914-16*)

Urgent. My men are on their last legs. I cannot keep some of them awake. They drop with their rifles in their hands and sleep in spite of heavy shelling. We are expecting an attack. Even that cannot keep some of them from dropping down.

Food and water has not reached us for two days, though have got by on rations of those killed … but must have water. I am alone with Phillips, who is wounded, and only a couple of sgts [sergeants]. Please relieve these men today without fail as I fear they have come to the end of their endurance.

The relieving force from the 3rd Division comprised the Norfolks, Berkshires and Royal Welch Fusiliers. When they advanced the enemy snipers in the wood allowed the first line through, then sniped the second and third lines. Two men of the Royal Welch Fusiliers showed uncommon valour and were each awarded the Victoria Cross.

Private Albert Hill bayoneted two of the enemy, then found himself cut off and surrounded by 20 Germans. He attacked them with bombs, killing and wounding many and scattering the remainder.

After returning to his lines he learnt that an officer and a scout were lying wounded in the wood. He assisted in bringing in the officer, while two others fetched the scout. He then captured two of the enemy. For his magnificent conduct Hill was awarded the Victoria Cross.

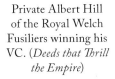

Private Albert Hill of the Royal Welch Fusiliers winning his VC. (*Deeds that Thrill the Empire*)

Corporal Joseph Davies and eight men became separated and were surrounded by the enemy. He managed to get his men into a shell hole, then by throwing bombs and rapid fire he routed the enemy and saw them off with the bayonet.

6.00pm: Three wounded officers, Lieutenant-Colonel Frank Thackeray, Sec-Lieut Edward Phillips and Sec-Lieut Garnet Green, with 140 men left the wood after being relieved by the Norfolk Regiment. They had been closer to the enemy than any other unit and had been continually under shell, bomb, machine-gun and rifle fire.

In July 1993 Willem Steenkamp wrote in the *Home Front*, the MOTH magazine:

> There are many personal accounts of the 1st Brigade's withdrawal from Delville Wood. One of the simplest, and best is the recollection of Private George Garnet Tanner of the 2nd Battalion, the Natal and Orange Free State Regiment, who recalled that as the last of the South Africans threaded their way out of the reeking wasteland of broken trees, shell holes and smashed biscuit boxes, the battle-hardened British troops who were moving in to take over Delville Wood looked at them, and wept.

(*The War Illustrated* Vol V)

So utterly depleted of energy were they that it took some time for them to realise that their battle was over. In the words of Corporal Sam Sumner of the 4th Battalion, the South African Scottish: 'Bone-weary, bewildered and confused, we pulled back … Only when we were picked up by the waiting trucks did we realise that we had been through the Valley of Death.'

No doubt many thoughts ran through their minds as they left Delville Wood behind them. I would guess that some were thinking only of deep, utter peaceful sleep, and others of food and drink, while still others had reached that stage of exhaustion where nothing mattered any more.

But I believe that more than one of them had only one overpowering thought in his mind, a thought that many a fighting soldier has had as he leaves the battlefield: 'Thank God, it's over and I'm alive'.

Some ex-soldiers I have spoken to still feel guilty that they should have had such a thought when so many of their friends had just died …

After six days of ceaseless shelling, bombing and machine-gun fire saturating that tiny forest, not even the trees survived. By night and day, every inch of that small area, only two kilometres square, was systematically bombarded with a barrage that at times reached 24,000 shells per hour. With every square metre of it churned and riddled and every crater filled with poison gas, how did anyone escape?

"Sheer luck," the old survivors said, "the whole area was the target, and we were in it."

Maurice Cristel (1st Bn D Coy) told the author that he survived by walking around looking for friends, thereby not staying in the same place long. The incorrigible old warrior died in 1983 while playing squash, aged 91. Eddie Fitz MM (2nd Bn HQ) commented drolly that Maurice had committed suicide.

Maurice Cristel aged 91. (*The Star*)

The British army historian, R E Johnston, wrote:

In all the records of war there could not be a story of more noble service than this which the South African Brigade rendered during those appalling six days. Here were not only the bombardments, the cross fire by hand guns, the grenade attacks, gas liquid fire and star shells, but bayonet charges, hand to hand combat and repeated forays by the tiny band that would not surrender until they had won. Yes, the South Africans won against enormous odds and at terrible cost, having beaten back wave after wave of enemy infantry …

… the rifles of the dwindling band of South Africans smoked and grew so hot that they could not be handled. The defenders threw them aside and used the rifles of the many dead who lay around them.

How did the dreadful battle come to happen? After two years of bitter trench warfare the Allies desperately needed reinforcements against fifty powerful German divisions on the eve of the Battle of the Somme. The South African Brigade arrived at Marseilles and were attached to [the] 9th Division, which was ordered to capture the heavily defended village of Longueval. The key to the conquest of Longueval was Delville Wood, to the east of the village, and the South Africans were ordered to take and hold the wood at all costs.

Under the command of General Tim Lukin, the South Africans took the wood on July 15th 1916. Then it became clear that they had been caught in a trap. The wood was soon surrounded by large forces of German infantry and artillery, who expected to wipe out the small South African contingent by nightfall, and retake the wood.

They kept trying, night and day, from July 15 to July 20. They threw everything they had at the South Africans – alternating bombardments with infantry charges, and every time they were beaten back they could not understand how anyone could survive such concentrated bombardments in a small area of such variety of attack, by gas, shell, machine-gun and rifle fire. They shelled every section of the wood, they riddled every angle of it with machine-guns, they poured in gas – and each time they moved in to clear away the dead a band of South Africans would charge them and throw them back, picking off their leaders with rifle fire.

After a final massive assault following the worst bombardment of the week, wave after wave of infantry were beaten back by a handful of South Africans, heavy-eyed with sleep, some wounded, some gassed, with the best marksmanship of that war, or any war. The Germans gave up, and on July 20th what was left of the South African Brigade handed over the wood to relieving British troops, who wept when they saw the remnant of the brigade marching from the shattered trees and churned earth of what had once been a forest.

The German Relief

According to Oberstleutnant Grautoff of IR 26 (Magdeburgers):

> At last on 20 July an order was received to stop further assault and hold the ground gained up to then. The regiment was completely exhausted and since the 19th I had been battling for relief. 41 officers had been lost, and the regiment's strength had shrunk to 10 officers and 358 men. The regiment was finally relieved by the 10th Company of the Grenadier Regiment No 12 on the 20th.

A German officer who visited the scene afterwards noted in his diary:

> The wood was a wasteland of shattered trees, charred and burning stumps, craters thick with mud and blood, and corpses, corpses everywhere. In places they were piled four deep. Worst of all was the lowing of the wounded. It sounded like a cattle ring at a spring fair.

10

Aftermath

According to L/Cpl Joey Pattison (1st Bn B Coy):

> When we got back to the old camp the General was there, waiting to see what was left of the SA Infantry Brigade. Well, out of about 4,500 only 700 returned – some 3,800 having been killed, wounded or missing – many lie under the soil in Delville Wood, having given their lives for the glory of South Africa and the British Empire …
>
> It took us three days before we could gather ourselves and then the General made us a speech and told us that they had expected Delville Wood to fall any minute in the five days we held it and the consequences would have been serious, but the General of the Division had given us the impossible to do and we had done it, and that for five days and nights we had been under bombardment that French critics said eclipsed anything at Verdun, and that we had had 9½ battalions of Prussian Guards against us and no one to reinforce us, and that he had always been proud of his Brigade and, if it was possible, he was still prouder.
>
> So next day we left the scene of the most ghastly experiences and sights I have ever seen, and, please God, may I never see again.

Lance/Corporal Frederick Charles Lee, 26, from Johannesburg was the sole surviving NCO of the Rand Light Infantry Company (3rd Bn C Coy). On 21 July he wrote:

> My Darling Mother,
> It is with a very sorrowful heart that I sit down to write you these few lines.
>
> We are a couple of miles behind the firing line now, having just come out of the Wood (Delville). After five days of absolute awfulness poor Angus Brown [Pte Harold Angus Brown, died of wounds 19 July 1916. Commemorated on Thiepval Memorial], my pal, died of wounds after about three hours awful suffering. He had both feet blown off by a shell on the 18th July.
>
> I wish you to let Mrs and Mr Brown know this. I saw him a little while after he was hit. He was quite conscious and showed real grit. He even asked me for a cigarette. I gave him a drink of water, and the only complaint he made at that time was, "My God, Fred, the pain is awful, and they can't give me anything to deaden it."

With that I ran down to the next dressing station and got the doctor to give me some morphia pills. When I got back to the dressing station in the wood Angus had been moved, and by the time I found him in another dressing station he was just about finished. I heard him say, "I wish the shell had killed me." I could not stop till the end, mother, as I had to go back to the front line, where we were being hard pressed.

Angus was a real hero. I had no idea he was going to die; he seemed so very cheerful. I've had a real good cry, I couldn't help it. When we got the order to get back to a certain rallying place, all we could muster of our company was 29. Out of the fine SA Brigade that went into action about 4,000 strong only approximately 300 are left. Of course quite a lot are wounded.

We have no officers left. Captain Jackson [Major John William Jackson] and Captain MacLachlan [Captain Donald Ronald MacLachlan] and two lieutenants killed, and the other two wounded. Not one officer of the 3rd Regiment has arrived so far [except Lieut-Col Thackeray].

I'm the only NCO in C Company who went into action left, and I'm only a lance-corporal and acting OC C Company. Now you can try and judge what we have gone through, and all just for a small wood.

You know what a wood looks like when the trees are in bloom – well, that is what it was like when we first drove them out. Since then they have continually bombarded it with hundreds and hundreds of guns, until now it is just like one or two poles stuck in the ground.

Yesterday they gave us ten solid hours bombardment with guns of all sizes and kinds – tear shells, gas shells, etc, and some *Jack Johnsons* [from the world champion American heavyweight boxer. Nickname of the German heavy shells exceeding 150mm] that threw you 30 yards away when they landed near you.

How I'm alive, mother, I can't say, and I am – I'm not ashamed to say it – one of many that prayed to get shot, absolutely worn out, nothing to eat or drink for two days, thanks to the enemy curtain fire, and no sleep for a week.

I'm going to turn in very soon for a well-earned rest. I haven't had a wash or a shave for three weeks, and my face is drawn so that I'll wager that I could stand in front of you for inspection and you would not know me. McCaffery [Lance-Corporal H D I McCaffery, taken prisoner] got a bad wound in the neck, whether he got out of the wood or not no one knows.

Also let Gracie know that young Rowe [Pte Walter Edmund Rowe, killed on 16 July 1916], whom I wrote to Vilma about some time ago, has also been killed. Also tell Katie that I've made enquiries about her cousin Fred and find that he and several others were blown to pieces by a shell. Give them all my love, mother, and tell them that I'm sorry that I can't write to them, but I am really too tired, can't keep my eyes open.

Goodbye, tons of love,

Fred.

Private Walter Giddy revelled in the peaceful back areas.

> 21st July. Had a bathe in the Somme and a change of underwear, now lying on the green hillside listening to our Division band, a happy day for the lads that were lucky enough to come through."
>
> 22nd July: ...General Lukin had us gathered round him, and thanked us for the splendid way in which we fought in Delville and Bernafay Woods. He said we got orders to take and hold the woods, at all costs, and we did for four days and four nights, and when told to fall back on the trench, we did it in a soldier like way. He knew his boys would, and he was prouder of us now, than even before, if he possibly could be, as he always was proud of South Africans. All he regretted was the great loss of gallant comrades, and thanked us from the bottom of his heart for what we had done.

When the remnant of his brigade paraded before Gen Lukin on 22 July he stood with bared head and tears running down his cheeks. Of the 3,155 officers and men on 14 July, 2,407 (77%) were casualties by 20 July, of whom 770 were killed or later died of wounds. He said:

> You see, I know the fathers and mothers of those lads. They're not just cannon fodder to me. I feel responsible for them to their parents.

(*The War Illustrated* Vol VII)

Frank Marillier had little to say about the parade:

> General Lukin thanked us for splendid gallantry of the SA boys and tells us how very proud he is, as the Battle of the Somme is the greatest battle on the British front and we took and held Delville Wood, which was the most important position the enemy had.
>
> Went for a bathe in the River Somme in the afternoon. Mail from mother and Mima.

On 23 July Lieut Fred English (1st Bn B Coy) wrote to his sister:

> My dearest Maud,
> Your letter received along with Violet's. Thanks for same. Letters have been rather scarce of late and when your two turned up I very nearly went frantic. We've been and am back.
>
> I feel sure you want to know all about it but you'll forgive me if I cut it all out. Memories will always be with me. My best pals amongst the officers and men have gone under. My feelings are vague. An intangible feeling of impossible loss.
>
> The fighting is a blank amidst hellish nightmares. You and Mona will realise how lucky I've been. Guardian angels must have been with me all along. There's not one amongst us (who has) not changed completely. New men with new ideas, tried and found good.
>
> I shall never get over their loss and don't know what to tell the mothers, wives and sisters of those under my charge.
>
> There's a glimmering hope of leave. Just think of the joy of it. Seeing civilians and speaking to friends again. We've been in pretty long now and can well do with a rest …
>
> Hopeless continuing letter as these poor chaps crop up. Can't realise that they're no more.
> Lots of love to you all,
> Fred.

On the 29th English wrote to Mrs Pattison about her son Victor:

> I feel sure you would like to know about your son, but fear it is extremely difficult to express the thoughts of deepest sympathy we all feel at your and our sad loss.
>
> He was a good young soldier and at all times the best of little gentlemen. He was killed in an attack on the enemy's trench: his death was instantaneous. The grave is marked and will never be forgotten by his comrades. We are all very proud of the mothers, sisters and wives at home. You are all so brave, far braver than those fighting.

Your son, C J, is doing well as lance-corporal, and promises to rise high, judging by his aptitude and keenness shown in everything he undertakes. We all long for dear old South Africa.

Kindest regards, etc.

On 2 August a London solicitor, Edgar Weldon, wrote to Vincent O'Riley in Cape Town:

My nephew Cyril Weldon gave me your name and address and asked me to write and let you know if anything should befall him.

I am sorry to say I have today received the sad news of his death on the 18th July. It is conveyed to me by cable from the military authorities in Cape Town and reads as follows: 'Notified Cyril Weldon Killed in Action in France 18th July. Kindly inform all relatives in England – Pentz.'

I do not at present know anything more. I have been very anxious for some time past as I saw his regiment was in the front and doing great work.

It is frightful this slaughter of all our nearest and dearest. There is hardly a house now which has not lost someone. If I get any further particulars I will write and let you have them.

Had he survived, Weldon would undoubtedly have been commissioned, as there was a great scarcity of officers after the battle. Virtually anyone who desired it, was commissioned.

The Wood

Fighting continued at Delville Wood on and off for the next eight weeks. The Germans counter-attacked on 31 August and regained a foothold. They were evicted on 8 September and on the 15th tanks were used for the first time in battle, starting at Delville Wood and reaching the village of Flers.

The wood was lost again during the massive German offensive of March/April 1918, but was retaken on 28 August 1918 for the last time. The war ended less than three months later on 11 November 1918.

In 1920, at the instigation of Sir Percy Fitzpatrick, the South African government purchased Delville Wood. A memorial was erected, which was unveiled by Gen Louis Botha's widow on 10 October 1926. The prime minister, Gen J B M Hertzog, addressed the gathering. The French government repurchased the wood then, in accordance with tradition, granted South Africa its use in perpetuity.

In 1986 the South African state president, Mr P W Botha, attended to open a museum at Delville Wood to honour all South Africans who had died in the 1st and 2nd World Wars and Korea.

In July 2014 the South African government arranged for the reinterrment of a Black South African soldier at Delville Wood. Private Myengwa Beleza of the South

African Native Labour Corps had been killed in France on 27 November 1916. Following the reburial ceremony Deputy President Cyril Ramaphosa laid a wreath at the French memorial.

The Wounded

Lieutenant Chauncey Reid experienced a typical evacuation from the front lines.

> The third time [he recalled anything] was in Corbie, about twelve miles behind the firing line. I must have been conscious for an hour or so this time, and wrote you [his mother] and Mrs Webster a field postcard.
>
> Then, off I went again and woke up in Rouen, where they cleaned out the wound and stitched it up. I was there, conscious nearly all the time, for about a day and a half, and then put in an ambulance. Phew! the throbbing of the engine was just grand!
>
> Then I was carried to the boat and to Southampton. Here an ambulance train whirled me to London, reaching there about five in the morning. Motor ambulances took us to the various hospitals. A crowd of us were sent to No 4 General …

(*Deeds that Thrill the Empire*)

I was placed in a great white ward, with twelve beds on each side. Beds with white sheets and nurses to look after us. Simply heaven! But Rouen was better, so far as pretty nurses went; but, unfortunately, at Rouen I wasn't taking much interest in life.

Anyhow, we were put to bed. We arrived bedecked with dockets – one telling what was the matter, the next your name, and so on. Presently the doctor came round and decided what was to happen to us and what treatment we were to have …

At the end of ten days the bandage over my eye was removed but my head was still tied up. I couldn't see out of the eye for two or three days, but it has gradually improved until it is almost normal now. The wound healed up wonderfully well and the bandages were taken off about a fortnight after I got in. Now there is very little to show where I was hit.

Altogether, we enjoyed the stay in hospital. Colonel Purcell called in one day, and Mrs Lukin and Mrs Dawson another. Mrs Wilson and the Websters turned up, so there were plenty of visitors. The only part I didn't like was that they would not allow me to get up. Not until the day before I left. That was about two weeks after I went in …

King George V visited a hospital ward and approached a middle-aged Afrikaner:

"Are you a Boer War veteran?" he asked.
  "Yes, sir", came the reply.
  "Whose side were you on?"
  "I fought against you, sir."
  "Why do you now fight for us?"
  "Because last time you were in the wrong, sir, but now you are in the right."

The king chuckled as he walked away.

Prisoners of War

The majority of the over 200 prisoners taken by the Germans were from the 3rd Battalion, who had defended the eastern side of the wood. Some of the 2nd Battalion POWs were captured during the initial taking of the wood. Most of them faced over two years of incarceration. A notable exception was Pte R Greener (2nd Bn) from Durban.

As he was severely wounded he was first sent to a hospital at Dulmen, thereafter to work in a quarry near Berlin. He escaped but was recaptured eight days later. He was then sent to Dusseldorf, on the Rhine.

Two months later he escaped again, this time with two friends, but was caught four days later at the Dutch frontier. His third attempt, when he escaped from a work party, was successful and he managed to reach Holland.

Greener provided much useful information to the War Office. He accepted a commission in the RAF and survived the war. The remainder of the prisoners were repatriated after the armistice.

The Brigade

The 1st SAI Brigade remained as part of the 9th Scottish Division for most of the war. In October 1916 they fought at the Butte de Warlencourt in the Somme, and suffered over 1,100 casualties – among those killed was Sandy Young VC. Lieutenant Edward Phillips and Sec-Lieut Jocy Pattison were mortally wounded.

The brigade was in action at Arras in April 1917. On the 12th at 4.30pm two companies of the 2nd SAI and two companies of the 4th SAI were marched down the main street of the village of Fampoux when, according to Cpl Arthur Betteridge (4th Bn C Coy) a Very light was fired:

> … instantly the most incredible barrage of shells fell on the men massed in the main road. Within minutes, half of them were casualties. We eventually found that only hours before we arrived, eight German light gun batteries had dug themselves in just behind the embankment which was an excellent observation point for them. I must truthfully say this brief bombardment was worse than any in Delville Wood while it lasted …

L/Cpl William Hewitt VC. (Ditsong National Museum of Military History)

Among the numerous Delville Wood veterans who were killed that day was 21-year-old L/Cpl Walter Giddy and Pte George Baker MM, who was with Faulds when he won the VC.

During the Third Battle of Ypres, on 20 September 1917, the brigade's second Victoria Cross was won by L/Cpl William Hewitt, also a Delville Wood survivor. The adjutant of the 1st Battalion, Captain Albert McDonald had a premonition that he would be killed, and he was.

During October 1917 they occupied a salient near Passchendaele, then the following month relieved the Guards Division at Gouzeacourt, in the Somme. In February 1918 they held a memorial service at Delville Wood.

On 23 March, during the massive German offensive, Captain Garnet

Green, the last man to leave Delville Wood on the 20th July, fought a rearguard action at Gauche Wood, where his company was overrun and he was killed. The author found a grave at nearby Gouzeacourt to an unknown South African captain, which is probably Green's.

Brigadier General Dawson commanded the brigade, nicknamed Dawson's five hundred, at the epic defence of Marrières Wood, 24 March 1918, only five miles from Delville Wood. Although surrounded and vastly outnumbered by the enemy his order to hold the wood at all costs were obeyed, until only one hundred men, without ammunition, were left to face a German brigade.

Dawson was forced to surrender, and confided in his diary,

> I cannot see that under the circumstances I had any option but to remain till the end. Far better to go down fighting against heavy odds than that it should be said we failed to carry out our orders. To retire would be against all the traditions of the service.

Major Heal and Captain Liebson were among the dead, while Lieutenant Mannie Faulds VC was among the officers captured. Corporal Gordon Smith was one of the wounded who were taken prisoner.

On 8 April 1918, the reconstructed brigade under Gen Tanner took part in the Battle of Messines Ridge and the Battle of the Lys. During June and July they fought at Meteren.

On 11 September the brigade joined the 66th Division. During October they fought from Beaurevoir to Mametz, then attacked the 'Hermann Line' and crossed the River Selle north of Le Cateau.

When the armistice was declared on 11 November the 1st SAI Brigade was at the forefront of the British advance. They had lost over 5,000 killed while in France – the equivalent of more than a brigade, a large price to pay by a small country.

Appendix I

Biographies

Ashworth, Pte Gwyn (1st Bn HQ)
In November 1916 Ashworth was commissioned in the field. He thereafter took part in battles at Arras, Ypres, Menin Rd and Passchendaele. He then joined the Royal Flying Corps. After coming top of his observer course, he was given a medical examination – and found to have an old scarred, perforated eardrum. He was discharged as unfit to fly, so in April 1918 joined the Indian Army. He was stationed at Ahmednagar until late 1919 when he was finally demobilised. He later married Myrtle Pocock. Ashworth died in 1978 aged 81 years.

Baker, Pte George Frederick (1st Bn A Coy)
He was badly wounded in assisting with the rescue of Lieut Craig, for which he was awarded the Military Medal. On 11 April 1918, two companies from the 2nd and 4th Battalions were ordered to march through the village of Fampoux. They were in full view of German artillery and dozens of machine-guns and were raked by fire. The casualties were 25 officers and 646 other ranks. George Baker was among those killed. General Allenby, who was in overall command, was recalled to England then given command of the Egyptian Expeditionary Force.

Betteridge, Private Arthur H (4th Bn C Coy)
He spent five months in hospital then returned to the front. As a signaller he was flown over the lines, then applied to transfer to the RFC. He learnt to fly and was commissioned in February 1918. Betteridge became a fighter pilot in No 3 Squadron. He strafed the German front line with his Sopwith Camel and was involved in a number of dog fights. On one occasion he buzzed an important football match, crash landed and had to be rescued from the irate crowd by senior officers.

He married Gladys Juniper in April 1919, returned to South Africa and his employment with the SA Railways. In 1921 he was a pallbearer at Andrew Proctor VC's funeral. He served at Air Force Headquarters during World War II, then became sales manager of SA Airways. Gladys died in July 1966. Betteridge lived in Pretoria, where he wrote *Combat in and over Delville Wood*. He died in January 1983 and was cremated.

Carstens, Private Jack (1st Bn D Coy)
He was commissioned, then wounded at Fampoux, wounded again at Messines, then transferred to the Indian Army for the duration. After serving with the Gurkhas he transferred to the north-west frontier as a captain, where a Pathan fortune-teller told him that he would find shiny stones someday. After five years in India he returned to South Africa.

His father, William, had found a deposit of gravel six miles south of Port Nolloth, which he thought might carry diamonds. Carstens prospected and in 1925 found the first diamonds in Namaqualand, but was later cheated out of them by a partner. Through this Dr Merensky came to the area and found the rich alluvial diggings at the mouth of the Orange River.

One day Carstens came across a Delville Wood comrade, "I took my fiancée to the old Tivoli in Darling Street, Cape Town and who should I meet but Robbie. He was all dressed up in Commissionaire's uniform complete with medals. He greeted me with 'By Gawd Sir, do you remember when I dug that funk hole for you in Delville Wood?'"

Carstens married Minnie Spiers from Uitenhage and had a son, Peter, in 1930. He remained on the alluvial diggings as a production manager, then retired to Cape Town. In 1962 he wrote 'A Fortune Through My Fingers'.

Catton, L/Cpl William (1st Bn A Coy)
After recovering in London he was selected to represent South Africa at the Lord Mayor's Show in London. Catton was commissioned and served in the 3rd Yorkshire Regiment. He was wounded by a shell blast while leading a working party in a trench near Ypres, but survived the war.

Congreve VC, Lieut-Gen William (XIII Corps HQ)
General Congreve was affectionately known as 'Old Concrete' by his men. He was created a KCB in 1917 and awarded the French Legion of Honour. After the war Sir Walter became governor of Malta, where he died on the 26th February 1927, aged 64.

Cooper, Drummer Henry (Harry) (3rd Bn C Coy)
He and seven other stretcher bearers were recommended for Mentions by Captain Liebson. In 1970, aged 73, Cooper lived in the Red Cross Ex-Servicemen's Home in Sandringham, Johannesburg.

Dawson, Lieut-Col Frederick Stuart (1st Bn HQ)
He commanded the Cape battalion at the Butte de Warlencourt in October 1916. Two months later Dawson was promoted temporary brigadier-general and commanded the brigade. He was captured when the brigade was overrun at Marrières Wood on 24

March 1918. His decorations included the CMG and DSO and bar. After the war he commanded the Returned Soldiers' Battalion. In 1920 he visited East Africa where he contracted enteric fever and died on 26 October.

English, Lieut Frederick William Hawthorne (1st Bn D Coy)
One of the few officers to survive the battle unscathed, he became OC of his company and was promoted captain. He married Edith Hawkins and they had no children.

His brother, Henry, married Dorothy Warneford, the sister of Flight Sub Lieutenant Reginald (Rex) Warneford VC, who had won the award on 7 June 1915, and died at Versailles on 17 June 1915.

Frederick English died at Humansdorp on 14 April 1974, and had his ashes scattered at the family graveyard at Robertson.

Faulds, Private William Frederick (1st Bn B Coy)
His Victoria Cross was gazetted on 9 September 1916. He was promoted corporal, then sergeant and commissioned in May 1917. He served in the Transport Department in Egypt briefly then returned to France. Lieutenant Faulds was captured when the brigade was overrun at Marrières Wood.

After the war he married Thelma Windell in Kimberley, where he was employed by De Beers as a mechanic. He rejoined the Kimberley Regiment as a captain and was in charge of guards of honour during royal tours.

Pte William Faulds VC. (Ditsong National Museum of Military History)

Faulds moved to Bulawayo. During World War II he served in Abyssinia and Egypt as a private in the Mechanical Corps. After the war he served as a government industrial inspector in Salisbury, where he died in August 1950, aged 55 years.

His medals were on display in the McGregor Museum in Kimberley, then sold to the Ditsong National Museum of Military History in Johannesburg, from where they were stolen. They have named one of their halls after him.

Featherstone, Sec-Lieut Clive (1st Bn B Coy)
He became a temporary captain in the Trench Mortar Battery and was wounded in October 1917 and March 1918. Featherstone served in Russia and was awarded a MC. He married Ivy Fitzhenry and had two daughters. His sister married his friend, Lieut Alfred Stuckey, who was also a Delville Wood survivor. Featherstone died at Port Elizabeth in 1967, aged 82.

Fitz, Private Eddie H (2nd Bn HQ)
Eddie Fitz and his two companions each earned the Military Medal for Bernafay Wood. Fitz later reconnoitred the Ypres front lines with Capt Garnet Green. He was

commissioned in March 1918, then due to a surplus of officers in the brigade transferred to the RAF for flight training.

He married Edeline Moore and had a son and a daughter, the latter dying when eight years old. During World War II Major Fitz was a personal staff officer to Major-General Frank Theron in the Middle East.

He returned to East London as a director of an electrical company, then in the early 1960's moved to Johannesburg. His wife died in 1974. After his death his son donated his medals to the East London MOTH Museum.

Giddy, Pte Walter (2nd Bn D Coy)
He was killed as a lance-corporal by shrapnel at Fampoux on 12 April 1917, and is commemorated by a memorial at Point-du-Jour Military Cemetery, Athies, France.

A friend of his, S G Phillips, wrote of him:

> Dear Gwen,
> I feel I must wrote and ask you to express to Walter Giddy's people my heartfelt sorrow at his death. I voice the opinion of everyone here that he was one of our best men. The day he was killed he was offered the job of looking after our overcoats in the Reserve Trenches while we went 'over the top', but he refused as he wanted to 'go over' with us. We were going through a village before the attack, when he fell dead from shrapnel. He was buried next day just outside the village and knowing him as I do both at college and here, I feel as if I have lost my best 'pal' here.
>
> I rejoined the regiment a few weeks ago [having been wounded at Bernafay Wood on 9 July 1916] after eight months in England, and he was just as cheerful as ever although a bit thinner, but this is not to be wondered at after spending a winter out here.
>
> If I can do anything for his people or you I shall be only too pleased. My address is D Company, 2nd SAI, France.
>
> Trusting that you are well, and with kind regards,
> I remain,
> Yours very truly,
> S G Phillips 1615.

Giddy's younger sister, Kate, transcribed his diary which her son, John Morris of Knysna, allowed the author to quote from.

Grautoff, Oberst Paul (IR 26)
Grautoff was promoted Oberst on 18 August 1916, and the following month was awarded the Knight's Cross. From February 1917 he was employed in various staff positions then joined the War Department. From September 1917 until September 1920 he was the commandant of Berlin, during which time he was promoted

major-general. Thereafter he commanded the Reichswehr – Brigade 5 until he retired from active service in March 1921. He died in Berlin on 8 February 1943, aged 74 years.

Green, Sec-Lieut Garnet G (2nd Bn C Coy)
He was awarded the Military Cross for Delville Wood and won a bar to the MC on 12 April 1917, for personally reconnoitring the front lines. He was promoted captain in January 1918, then was killed while defending Gauche Wood during the German offensive of 21 March 1918. He is commemorated on the Pozières Memorial.

Lieut Garnet Green MC.
(Brian K Thomas)

Grimsdell, Private Robert 'Bob' (4th Bn)
He survived his neck wound and was repatriated.

> At the end of the war I returned to Johannesburg and looked up an old comrade – Foreman Carpenter, Johannesburg Municipality. I had grown a moustache and had filled out a bit. 'What's your name?' he asked:
> 'Bob Grimsdell, surely you know that', I replied. 'Now look', said my old comrade, 'I'm sick and tired of you bums coming the old soldier trick and trying to make an easy quid, you just f… off before I throw you out – it happens that I was next to Bob Grimsdell when he was killed at Delville.'
> So I just went. Our family joke – 'Were you in Delville Wood?' 'Yes, I was killed there'.

Grindley, Pte David (1st Bn C Coy)
He was hospitalised and his legs amputated. After the war when the troop train arrived at Kimberley he sat on a 44 gallon drum and shouted, "You bastards! You left me for dead. You bastards! You left me to die."

His former comrades were surprised and pleased to see that he hadn't been killed in the wood. Douglas Bader visited him on one of his trips to South Africa.

Hill, Captain Eustace St C (1st Bn Padre)
He was severely wounded at the Butte de Warlencourt and lost his right arm. Though awarded the MC, he never wore it. In April 1917 he returned to the Front, then in March 1918 was taken prisoner at Marrières Wood. After the war he became headmaster of St John's College, Johannesburg. His last years were spent at a monastery in Hampshire, where he died in 1953 aged 80 years.

Kirkman, Sidney Frank (1st Bn C Coy)
He had been severely wounded by shrapnel in the
right arm and shoulder. After recuperating he joined
the Royal Field Artillery, was commissioned and later
became a captain.

His parents refused to believe that his brother Alf
was dead [Killed on 18 July], believing that he was a
prisoner somewhere in Germany. However, many years
later they received a letter from a German soldier, who
said that he had retrieved Alf's pocket book from his
jacket during the battle. His parents finally came to
terms with the hard truth.

Doug had been wounded during the battle and
taken prisoner by the Germans.

Captain S F Kirkman.
(P Kirkman)

Knibbs, Sec-Lieut Arthur (2nd Bn D Coy)
Arthur Knibbs survived the battle and was evacuated
to the 4th London General Hospital in Denmark Hill.
London, where he wrote:

> … the sister tells me that I am doing famously, my
> wound is healing up very well indeed … Yesterday I
> got up for the first time. I have had quite a number
> of S[outh] Africans in to see me, they have been
> awfully good to me. I must hurry up, for the Sister
> has started the dressings (the butcher shop I call it).

He later returned to South African to marry his
fiancée, Florence.

Lee, L/Cpl Frederick Charles (3rd Bn C Coy)
He was commissioned after Delville Wood and was
killed near Arras on 9 April 1917. Lee is buried in the
St Nicolas British Cemetery, north of Arras.

Loubser, Pte Albert Johannes (1st Bn D Coy)
He was awarded the DCM for his bravery in saving
lives at Delville Wood. He was later promoted
corporal. On 12 October 1917, he was wounded in
the back at Ypres. Lieutenant Geoffrey Lawrence was
called by an officer to a dressing station.

Arthur Knibbs and his wife.
(Knibbs Family)

We have a dying man whom we can hardly understand. Will you come and do what you can for him?

Lawrence complied, I went in and there was poor Loubser, one of our staunchest company stretcher-bearers with a terrible wound in his left shoulder and going fast from loss of blood and shock. I stayed with him a while and comforted him, speaking in Afrikaans until he lost consciousness and died a short while later …

Poor old Loubser, the finest and most reliable stretcher-bearer in our company. A great strapping Afrikaans speaking lad from the Western Province who had been with us from the very start and who when he signed on in early 1915 could barely speak a word of English.

He is buried at the Dozingham British Cemetery, north of Poperinghe, Belgium.

Liebson, Captain/Dr Stephen (3rd Bn HQ)
Although wounded Stephen Liebson continued attending to the wounded until the 19th July, for which he earned the Military Cross. He was killed when the brigade was overrun at Marrières Wood on 22 March 1918.

Captain Stephen Liebson. (*South Africa Magazine*)

Lukin, Brig-Gen Henry Timson (1st SAI Bde HQ)
Brigadier Lukin commanded the brigade at the Butte de Warlencourt. In December 1916 he was promoted major general and given command of the 9th Scottish Division. He relinquished command in March 1918 due to his wife's illness, then returned to command the 64th Highland Division. He was awarded a CB then in 1917 created a KCB.

General Lukin retired from the army in 1919 as his health was affected by the gas he'd breathed in at Delville Wood. He died on 15 December 1925, aged 65, and is buried in the Plumstead Cemetery, Cape Town. A statue of him stands in the City Gardens.

Marillier, Private Leander Francis Henri (2nd Bn C Coy)
Frank Marillier was commissioned in October 1916. He was shot through the chest at Fampoux, but survived and served in the Second World War. He farmed near Queenstown and died there in May 1976, aged 81.

Maskew, Private Frank (1st Bn M-G)
He was promoted lance-corporal. On 19 September he wrote to his little sister, May:

This terrible war will soon be over. It can't last much longer now and then you'll have me home again. That will be a great day when we all come home again. Yet it'll be a sad day for us all because Allan [their brother who was killed in the East African campaign] won't be there. Still you must know May that there are many other little sisters and brothers who have also lost their brothers and that in our brigade scarcely a day passes but that some fellows have to lay down their lives, and mothers and other dear ones are suddenly made very sad. Don't you sometimes feel very proud that you have a brother who has sacrificed his life in this great cause?

Frank Maskew.
(Mrs P McCarthy)

He may have had a premonition, for within two weeks he lay in a shell hole at the Butte de Warlencourt. A hand grenade rolled into the hole and he picked it up to throw when it exploded, shredding his hand. Maskew lay there all day until taken to a sap where a doctor was selecting cases to operate on. He was ignored as a terminal case, so decided, "Buggar it! I'm not going to die." He ended up at a Casualty Clearing Station where his hand was amputated from the mid-arm.

Maskew was sent to No 6 General Hospital at Rouen, then to Richmond Hospital in London. He struggled to write with his left hand, managing to scrawl letters home. He returned to South Africa in January 1918.

Maskew became a clerk in the Cape Provincial Education Department. He married Enid Fischer and attended many Delville Wood reunions. Maskew often quoted Shakespeare and his grandson became a Shakespearian actor with CAPAB. He died in 1983, aged 91 years.

Meredith, Private Dudley (3rd Bn C Coy)
He escaped from the Dulmen POW Camp with two Australians, but was recaptured when only four kilometres from the Dutch border. After the war he studied agriculture at Potchefstroom and in the USA. He married and had two children before his wife was killed in a motor accident. He then entered the ministry and qualified as a D Sc in 1947. He wrote a book on grasses of South Africa and died on 3 July 1975, aged 79.

Miller, Captain Allister M (Royal Flying Corps)
He was promoted flight commander and awarded the DSO for the Somme. At the end of 1916 he embarked on a recruiting drive in South Africa. One of his recruits was Andrew Proctor, who was to win a VC, DSO, DFC, MC and Bar.

In 1919 Miller did the first internal commercial flight in South Africa. He became a member of parliament in 1924. During World War II Lieut-Col Miller commanded air training schools. He died in Port Elizabeth on 14 October 1951, aged 59.

Noack, Lieut Anno Ludwig (5th Garde Feld Artillerie)
During the war he was awarded the Iron Cross, 1st Class, for leading his unit to safety after they had been surrounded. He later served as a gas officer of the 3rd Garde Infanterie Division.

After the war Noack studied at Dresden, then specialized in mining engineering to earn a doctorate. After being a director of a Silesian coalmine, he emigrated to South Africa in 1931. He lived in Cape Town and in 1966 recorded his Delville Wood experiences. Noack died in September 1973, aged 82.

Pattison, L/Cpl Charles Joseph (1st Bn B Coy)
Joey Pattison was commissioned and rejoined the 1st Battalion. On 16 October he wrote to his parents:

> Well we are back again in the midst of roaring guns. Away on our right is Delville Wood where Vic and so many boys lie. We can see the charred sticks and stumps of Montauban and Trônes Wood, and now we are moving into the thick of it all again. However, I have always put my trust in my Maker, and if he wills, I shall come safely through, and if not, remember we shall all meet again, and I shall be with Vic. Love to all, Au revoir!
>
> Your aff[ectionate] son, J.

Sec-Lieut Joey Pattison.
(Justice K Satchwell)

Within days he was mortally wounded at the Butte de Warlencourt. He was severely wounded in both legs, left arm and right eye and his wounds became septic as he lay out for a few days in No Man's Land before being brought in. He reached Rouen's No 8 General Hospital on 24 October. Padre Hill was a patient and commented that Pattison's infectious humour soon had the nurses laughing. He died after an operation that day.

Phillips, Sec-Lieut Edward J (3 SAI attd SA LTMB)
He was awarded a Military Cross for Delville Wood in September 1916. Phillips was mortally wounded at the Butte de Warlencourt on 13 October 1916. He was evacuated to the Dernancourt XV Corps Main Dressing Station, southwest of Albert, where he died on the 16th and is buried there. He left his wife, Annie, a son Edward and a daughter Myrtle in East London.

Lieutenant Edward Phillips. (Ditsong National Museum of Military History)

Reid, Lieut Chauncey (1st Bn D Coy)

He was evacuated via Corbie and Rouen to London's No 4 General Hospital. His head wound healed and he returned to command his old company from 16 December 1916. He found that his old platoon had suffered 57 casualties out of 62 at Delville Wood. In July 1917 Reid joined the Royal Flying Corps and was gazetted a Temporary Second-Lieutenant.

On 4 January 1918, he was forced down behind enemy lines and captured, then incarcerated near Karlsruhe. Despite attempting to tunnel his way out he was eventually freed after the Armistice. Reid remained with the Army of Occupation until July 1919, then returned to South Africa in the *Balmoral Castle* in September.

Reid married and farmed near Knysna. He and his wife Katie named one of their sons 'Nimmo' after his dead friend. He died on 12 August 1970, and is buried at Knysna. A stained glass window to his and Katie's memory is in the local St George's Anglican Church.

Samuels, Joseph (3rd Bn)

He was wounded in the arm and back and evacuated to Richmond Hospital in London. After returning to the Front he was meant to push a stalled truck with shells on it, but it blew up before he could! At Arras he was hit in the eye and shoulder by shrapnel.

After being at the Stoke Newington Hospital he convalesced at Brighton, then returned to fight at Ypres. During the attacks on pillboxes he threw grenades through the loopholes until he was severely wounded. He was invalided home on the *Galway Castle*, but it was torpedoed on 12 September 1918. Joe Samuels was among the few survivors. He was at Crewe on Armistice Day.

Joe Samuels, 99, probably the last survivor of Delville Wood, with the author on 23 April 1997. (I Uys)

Samuels returned to live in Cape Town, where he owned the New Globe Cinema in Woodstock, then moved to the United States. He was living at Fort Lauderdale when, aged 90 in 1988, he visited Cape Town.

He returned nine years later with his lawyer grand-daughter and the author was privileged to interview him. He recalled the indecision in the south-east corner as to whether the men they faced were French or German. His daughter was astonished when the author confirmed that his old tale was quite true. He died in March 1998, aged 100.

Smith, Pte Gordon (1st Bn B Coy)

He wrote to his brother, Denzil, and sister, Ann, during the war. After recuperating he fought at the Butte de Warlencourt and other battles. On 22 March 1918, during the German offensive, he was wounded, taken prisoner and sent to the POW camp at Zerbst.

Gordon Smith. (E Badenhorst)

After the war he returned to work for the SA Railways at Port Elizabeth. He married Suzanne 'Kitty' Moolman and they later adopted her cousin, Jacoba 'Toodles' du Preez, who was orphaned when her parents died in the 1918 influenza epidemic.

Smith served as a warden and on the council of the Holy Trinity Church. He was a member of the St John's Ambulance for 47 years in which he served as assistant commissioner.

From 1943 Gordon Smith was manager and secretary of the Stella Londt retirement complex, of which Kitty was matron. It burnt down on 22 December 1965. Kitty, 65, was so distraught that she died of a heart attack. He died on 19 January 1974, aged 79 and was cremated at the South End Crematorium.

Stuart, Private Charles B (2nd Bn C Coy)

Charlie Stuart was imprisoned in the Dulmen Camp, then in February 1917 moved to the Sprotau POW Camp. His brother, Walter, joined the 2nd Battalion and was taken prisoner at Marrières Wood in March 1918.

After the war Stuart worked at the ABC Bank in Durban. By 1925 he was the Mooi River branch manager, where he married Norah Lawrence. During World War II he served as an officer in the Natal Reserve battalion. He later worked at Umzinto and Port Shepstone, then retired to Pietermaritzburg in 1954.

On his deathbed he told his nephew, Bob Stuart, how he regretted having shot the young German. He died on 22 May 1972, aged 77. Another nephew, Kelsey Stuart, became president of the SA Red Cross and chief legal adviser to the SA Associated Newspapers.

Stuckey, Lieut Alfred Jeremiah (1st Bn)
He came from British Columbia, Canada, and served in the Cape Mounted Rifles during the Boer War. Stuckey had been buried a number of times during the bombardment. He married Clive Featherstone's sister, became a farmer and water driller, and was a trick rider in Texas Jack's Wild West circus, with Will Rogers. He was fatally injured in a motor car accident in Parow, Cape Town, on 31 March 1939.

Tanner, Private George Garnet (2nd Bn D Coy)
Garnet Tanner was among the last 143 men to leave the wood. He was awarded the DCM for his bravery in Delville Wood. After marrying he returned to South Africa in April 1919. He was one of a Kaffrarian Rifle platoon inspected by the king in 1947. When he saw the DCM medal he stopped to speak to Tanner and enquired how he had won it. They later lived in Bergvliet, near Cape Town.

They had a daughter, Jean, whose husband was a captain in the merchant navy who was awarded the DSM, and a son, Bert. The latter served with the Railway Unit in Egypt and Italy and attended the Ceremony at Delville Wood in 1996.

His brother Douglas won the MM at Ypres and served in Egypt during World War II. Stanley lived in London and served in the Home Guard during the Second World War. His son, Bobby, served as a captain with the artillery in Burma. Another son, Punch, trained as a pilot at Irene, Transvaal, then was shot down over Europe and killed.

Tanner brothers: Standing – Stanley and Garnet DCM. Seated Doug MM. (A Tanner)

Tanner, Lieut-Col William E C (2nd Bn HQ)
He was awarded a DSO and promoted temporary brigadier-general for Delville Wood. After fighting at Arras Tanner commanded the 8th Brigade of the 3rd Division. He returned to command the 1st SAI Brigade after Marriere's Wood in March 1918. At war's end he had a CB and CMG as well.

Tanner thereafter held important posts in the Union Defence Force. He attended the 1926 unveiling of the Delville Wood Memorial. Twelve years later he led the SA Battlefields Pilgrimage to Europe. During World War II he was OC of Wit Command and Cape Command. He then farmed at Elgin, Cape, where he died on 29 September 1943, aged 67.

Thackeray, Lieut-Col Edward Frank (3rd Bn HQ)
He was recommended for the Victoria Cross for his dogged defence of Delville Wood, but received a DSO, and later a CMG. He commanded the 3rd Battalion until its disbandment in February 1918. Thackeray died in Johannesburg in 1956, aged 86. His daughter, Meg van der Westhuizen, was of great assistance to the author in providing him with the messages which had been sent during the battle.

Thomson, Actg/CSM James (2nd Bn C Coy)
He had fought on grimly, refusing to retire and was among the 140 men who left the wood on the 20th. He was commissioned and awarded the DCM for conspicuous gallantry. On 12 October 1916, Thomson led his platoon at the Butte de Warlencourt and was grievously wounded in the head, from which he died five days later.

Von Wuthenau, Oberst Karl Adam Ludwig J T (RIR 107)
He was decorated with the Knight's Cross of the Military St Heinrich's Order. In May 1917 he was appointed commander of 48 Reserve Infantry Brigade on the Eastern Front. From 1 July Russian artillery bombarded them and they were forced back, but after tenacious fighting they regained the lost terrain. For this Von Wuthenau was made Commander 2nd Class of the Military St Heinrich's Order.

At the end of 1917 he and his brigade were transferred to the Western Front. They fought at Cambrai, then took part in the March offensive. They fought in various engagements until the armistice, then he led them home in 1918 as a major-general. In 1926 he was promoted lieut-general.

He became heir to his father's estate of Hohenthurm, near Halle, East Germany, and a member of the German Gentlemen's Club. His wife died in 1930 and in 1937 he married a commoner, Dorothea Wolff. Von Wuthenau died at Halle on 13 November 1946, aged 83 years.

Wepener, Private Victor (3rd Bn B Coy)
While a prisoner of war he escaped from a work party but was recaptured. During World War II Major Wepener served with the Imperial Light Horse at Bardia. Though shot in the leg he continued directing the fighting until nightfall, for which he earned the DSO. He commanded the Imperial Light Horse from 1948 to 1953. He revisited Delville Wood in 1966 and 1986 with South African contingents.

While on a flight back to South Africa from the latter visit he was invited by the State President, Mr P W Botha, to sit in first class. He declined, saying that he wished to remain with his friend, Ian Uys. The author has never forgotten that honour, nor that of seeing at his death bed a copy of the bible and the author's book about him in Delville Wood entitled 'Rollcall'.

Woolf, L/Cpl Maurice (SA Light Trench Mortar Battery)
He was later commissioned and ended the war as a captain. Woolf returned to his family farm and in 1922 received a Digger's Certificate. Five years later he married Anna Grundlingh and had a daughter, Joan. In 1928 he received a Diamond Dealer's Licence. In 1938 Anna became a nurse at the Krugersdorp Hospital. Woolf served as an administrative officer during World War II. He managed cattle ranches in Botswana, where he was friends with the ruling Khama family, until his death in 1966.

Young VC, Lieut Alexander 'Sandy' (4th Bn D Coy)
Young was invalided to a hospital in Brighton. He had assisted the German authorities in South West Africa during the 1904 Herero uprising, for which he was awarded an Iron Cross. On the outbreak of the First World War he publicly burnt it. He must surely be the only man to have worn the VC, the Iron Cross and the Legion of Honour!

He recuperated at Galway, Ireland, before returning to the Front, where he led his platoon at the Butte de Warlencourt and was killed. His name is commemorated on the Thiepval Memorial to the missing.

His VC was acquired by Lord Ashcroft for his VC Trust Collection. The author who owned his Natal 1906 medal sold it to the Trust.

Lieut Alex 'Sandy' Young.
(*The War Illustrated* Vol VII)

Appendix II

An Overview

Anzac and Africander in Action

By Edward Wright. *The War Illustrated* 19th August 1916.

Sir Douglas Haig gave an inspiring Imperial touch to his operations by detailing an Australian Division to attack the German bastion of Pozières, while the South African Brigade advanced into the other German bastion at Delville Wood. Both horns of our advancing crescent were thus formed by the splendid fighting men from the Overseas Divisions – the Anzacs, hardened and tempered n Gallipoli; the Africanders, inured to warfare in the deserts of German South-West Africa and Egypt.

But the German Commander-in-Chief employed the pause in our attack in the two days of mist and rain [16th and 17th] to prepare a tremendous counter-blow. It is clear he no longer regarded our New Army as an army of amateurs. He brought up against our men the pick of all the finest forces of Prussia. As he proclaimed to the world, the Brandenburgers, who had stormed Fort Douaumont, were brought from behind Verdun towards Delville Wood. Then the Prussian regiments of Magdeburg were brigaded with the Brandenburgers, who were further strengthened by large fresh forces of Saxons and the remains of two broken divisions of the Prussian Guard.

Hundreds of additional heavy guns were sited around the Delville-Longueval position, and in some places 13,000 troops gathered for the attack on a front of 2,000 yards. It was the first time since the opening battle of the Somme that the enemy had really counter-attacked, and he certainly succeeded in putting a terrific weight into his blow.

All day Delville Wood looked like a stretch of subterranean fire. The trees were blotted out by a pall of smoke, and through the smoke came jets and spits of flame, caused by bursting shells. Then at half-past five in the evening three great Prussian and Saxon columns advanced on the three sides of Delville Wood against the South Africans, while other Prussian forces attacked the South Africans and Highlanders in Longueval, Waterlot Farm and near Guillemont.

Near Guillemont our troops joined the famous French corps which contained the Iron Division, and the principal aim of the German commander was to cut through Delville Wood and make a deadly disorganising gap between the British and French armies. The brunt of the attack fell upon the South Africans.

They were blinded with bromide shells, poisoned with gas shells, burnt with liquid flame shells, and annihilated by huge high-explosive shells which made forty-feet craters. Our hastily improvised trenches in the wood were wiped out, and the South Africans were forced back in small broken bands to a reserve trench held by the Highlanders.

This trench was as weak as those that had been lost. There had been no time to construct elaborate deep dug-outs, and the enemy's shells had blown away half the sandbags. If the little weak force of South Africans and Highlanders had made a stand in the trench they would have been wiped out. They would also have been wiped out had they tried to retire through the enemy's curtain of fire on their rear.

They charged forward [at Longueval]. It was one of the finest feats in the whole war. Fragments of battalions, scraps of companies, shreds of platoons – they rallied and swept forward in sheer, desperate desire to die fighting. But by getting into a mad, stabbing, hand-to-hand combat with the German troops in the mazy screen of trees, they not only avoided the German shell fire, but strangely picked up reinforcements as they went on.

One South African, the only man left out of a Lewis-gun team, came up with his gun at a very critical moment, swept a large force of the enemy back, and wiped out one of their machine-gun parties. Then another advance party of South Africans was found still holding out on the edge of the wood, by an open drive known as Buchanan

A Lewis-gun Team. (Ditsong National Museum of Military History)

Street. As they were despairingly fighting against a ring of flame, the ring was broken by the extraordinary charge of the remnants of the South Africans and Highlanders, who thus obtained further reinforcements.

All night the battle went on, and all the next day and the next. The enemy's curtain of fire on our rear made it difficult to bring up British reinforcements, but they slowly filtered through the barrage of gas shells, liquid flame shells and 'Jack Johnson' shells. So the line through the wood and Longueval village, won back by the South Africans and the Highlanders, was held and gradually strengthened.

The South Africans were withdrawn from the position they had captured, after fighting for five days and nights and leaving the flower of their brigade in the wood they called Devil's Wood. The Highlanders were also relieved after six days and nights of the most bloody struggle in history.

Many of the relieving battalions were formed of men recruited under the Derby Group System. When they went into the fight in Delville Wood on July 20th they were called Derby's Men. When they came out of the wood on July 31st they were called Derby's Devils. They had taken all Delville Wood, stormed the last enemy stronghold in Longueval, and broken up innumerable German counter-attacks. By their achievement the right flank of the German second line was definitely conquered, allowing our dominating centre at High Wood to be again advanced to the high part of the ridge.

This extremely important movement on the High Wood-Longueval-Delville Wood sector was greatly helped by the Anzac advance on the Pozières side of our line …

Appendix III

Poems

To honour the men of Delville Wood

What tongue can tell the tale of Delville Wood,
How to the last the gallant Springboks stood
And faced a foe of overwhelming might
Fighting through day, and sleepless through the night
Three times the sun in splendour rose and set
In scenes no man could live through and forget
Three times the sacred silence of night
Fled from the discords of that ghastly fight.
The order came on that first fateful hour
To those dear lads – the glory and the flower
Of brave South Africa – to take the wood
To every man the cry came where he stood
Take it and hold it at whatever cost
Thank heaven they took it; not one trench was lost.
Took it and held it, though the fiendish Huns
Rained fire incessant from their devilish guns
Nobly they fought – and fell – all undismayed
Though God alone knew what the price they paid
And only the recording angel's pen
Can write with justice of those glorious men
Who through the eternity of seven long hours
Of fierce bombardment – crushed and torn like flowers
Beneath a grindstone pressed on either flank
Met and hurled back three regiments rank on rank
And e'er the third day's sun in glory set
The fiery Brandenburgers these heroes met
And gathering up their failing strength at last
Then in the trenches where their young life's blood

Ran like a river in the crimson flood
Three deep they dropped asleep – their last long sleep
With scarce a handful left alive to weep
Those tears of pride which comrades of the brave
Shed unashamed on many a soldier's grave
So Delville Wood was taken – aye and held
And in their deaths those noble lads excelled
All that the bards have ever sung and poets said
Honour, South Africa, your gallant dead.

Driver O'Neill,
SA Infantry.

Delville Wood

In Delville Wood the larches grow
And poplar striplings slim,
The Hazel boughs made tracery
Against the sky's blue rim;
And very fair the summer's mood
In far-off, unknown Delville Wood.

In Delville Wood no poplars stand
In Delville Wood no larches grow:
Nature, bewildered and aghast,
Lies mutilated, bleeding, low –
For blossomed sanctuary is left
Red wreckage of all life bereft.

Yet in its rain and despair
Has come to Delville Wood a fame,
Graven for evermore on hearts
That erstwhile had not heard its name,
Made deathless now by those who stood
And fought and died in Delville Wood.

O little wood in far-off France!
By what strange ways their feet were led,
Our sons, of different tongue and race,
Who there upon your pathways red,
One in true-hearted fortitude,
Forged living links of brotherhood.

And the deep wounds of Delville Wood
For e'er on our Scroll shall flame,
With sacrificial light that fades
Old scars of bygone grief and shame;
So for all time shall Delville Wood
Stand unto us as Holy Rood.
                    B M Bromley
                    Kalk Bay.

Painting 'Delville Wood' by Sir William Orpen.
(Durban Museum and Art Gallery)

DELVILLE WOOD – July 1916

Stark in the smoking forest the blackened tree trunks stood,
Grimly pointing skywards, relics of Delville Wood.
Three thousand Springboks died there. Their battle was not lost.
Bravely they did their duty, and counted not the cost.
They fought for an ideal, 'The war to end all wars.'
Did they die in vain? Was this a lost cause?
Not while we remember the sacrifice they made.
The story of their courage, will never, never fade,
Yet still the carnage goes on, all across the world,
For 'Freedom' or 'Religion' banners are unfurled.
When will we learn our lesson, that all men should be free?
When will we learn to live together, all in harmony?
Remember how those heroes stood there side by side,
Boer and Brit, they bravely fought and just as bravely died.
This is their example, their legacy to follow.
If we just ignore it, their sacrifice is hollow.
This day as we remember the men of Delville Wood,
Let us not forget the ideals for which they stood.

Pat Stannard
Battleaxe Shellhole, Port Alfred
July 1993

Delville Wood, October 1918. (Author's collection)

Appendix IV

German regimental histories

___

The Reserve Infantry Regiments

The RIR 106 and RIR 107 were part of the south support troops who clashed with South African troops in Trônes Wood, eastern and southern Delville Wood and at the Sugar Factory.

The RIR 106 had been called up from various reserve troops on mobilization in the Eastern German province of Saxony. The regiment was sent to the Western Front where it fought at the Marne, the Aisne, Loos, Hollebeke, Yser Canal, Vimy and Hill 60 at Ypres.

The RIR 106 was part of the 123rd Infantry Division which came under command of the VI Reserve Korps on 7 July 1916. At first it was intended to use the whole 123rd ID for a concerted attack along the Somme front. However, the critical position on the front forced the general command to withdraw this order. Instead, the individual troops were ordered to support critical positions as the need arose.

The 12th Reserve Division and the 22nd Reserve Infantry Brigade both made use of the RIR 106, ordering battalions in to support troops of the IR 178 and IR 182, who were attempting to hold Trônes Wood. Other battalions went into position along the Second Line, the Braune Stellung.

The RIR 107 had been formed at mobilization from reserve and 'Landwehr troops in Leipzig. They were ordered into action in France and fought at Givet, the Marne, Champaigne, Moronvilliers and Auberive. On 21 May 1916, Oberst Graf Wuthenau took over command of the regiment. From 1 June he also commanded the brigade, under XII Reserve Corps.

The Reserve Infantry Regiment 99 from Strassburg and Zabern in the Alsace was placed in the 3rd Line, which stretched from Ginchy to Foureaux Wood and lay between Longueval and Flers. The regiment consisted mainly of Westfalian workers from the coalmines and factories, from the Rhineland and Baden, and about 100 from the Alsace, many of whose fathers had fought in the French Army in 1870.

At the beginning of the war they were in action in the Alsace and the Vosges Mountains. Thereafter they fought at the Ancre, followed by Arras, Serre and Fricourt.

Relaxing prisoners. (Ditsong National Museum of Military History)

The RIR 99 was at Thiepval up to 8 July, and was directly involved in holding it at the time that La Boiselle fell to the English. After a few days rest they were moved to the 2nd and 3rd Lines at Flers.

The IR 153 (Altenburgers)

The IR 153, from Central Germany, was a regiment rich in tradition, whose prehistory went back into the mists of the middle ages. The regiment took part in many famous battles in the 17th and 18th century. It was the eighth regiment in the Thüringian contingent, under command of the Prussian Army. '153' denotes the number of the regiment within the hierarchy of the Prussian Army.

There was a sensation when at mobilization for the Great War, the Duke of Sachsen-Altenburg disregarded his position as ruler of his duchy and lieutenant-general, by requesting and being granted active command of his regiment.

The regiment had fought at Mons, Le Cateau, the Marne, Aisne, Arras, La Bassee and Loos and had just spent eight months in position at Lens when ordered on 6 July to march to the Somme.

The IR 72 (Thüringians)

The Royal Prussian 4th Thüringian IR 72 had been created in 1859 as the 32nd Landwehr IR and renamed a year later. The regiment was in reserve during the war against Denmark in 1864. Two years later it fought in several of the civil war battles. Its greatest losses, however, were due to an outbreak of cholera.

During the Franco-Prussian War the regiment attained fame when on 16 August, 1870, it distinguished itself at the Battle of Vionville. Over 40 years later it was mobilized for the Great War on 2 August 1914. The Thüringians fought at Quievrain, Le Cateau and Framerville that month, then at the Aisne, Arras and Monchy. In 1915 from June to August it was at the battle of Loretto Heights and thereafter at Loos until required for the Somme in July 1916.

Appendix V

British Order of Battle

British Expeditionary Force	Gen Sir D Haig
2nd Army – in Flanders	Gen Sir H Plumer
3rd Army – at the Somme	Gen Sir E Allenby
4th Army – at the Somme	Gen Sir H Rawlinson
6th Army (French) – at the Somme	Gen M E Fayolle

Fourth Army

III Corps	Lieut-Gen Sir E Pulteney
VIII Corps	Lieut-Gen Sir A G Hunter-Weston
X Corps	Lieut-Gen Sir T L N Morland
XIII Corps	Lieut-Gen Sir W N Congreve VC
XV Corps	Lieut-Gen Sir H S Horne

XIII Corps

3rd Division	Maj-Gen J A Haldane
9th Division	Maj-Gen W T Furse
18th Division	Maj-Gen I Maxse
30th Division	Maj-Gen J Shea

9th Division

26th Brigade	Brig-Gen A B Ritchie
8th Black Watch	
7th Seaforth Highlanders	
5th Cameron Highlanders	
10th Argyll & Sutherland Highlanders	

27th Brigade   Brig-Gen S W Scrase-Dickens
11th Royal Scots
12th Royal Scots
9th Scottish Rifles
6th King's Own Scottish

1st S A Infantry Brigade   Brig-Gen H T Lukin
1st Battalion (Cape)
2nd Battalion (Natal, OFS, Border)
3rd Battalion (Transvaal, Rhodesia)
4th Battalion (SA Scottish)
28th Bde Machine Gun Company

Appendix VI

1st SA Infantry Brigade

Headquarters Brig-Gen H T Lukin CMG DSO

1st Battalion Cape Lieut-Col F Dawson
A Coy Western Cape Capt P Jowett
B Coy Eastern Cape Capt G Miller
C Coy Kimberley Capt H Jenkins
D Coy Cape Town Major E Burges

2nd Battalion Natal, OFS & Border Lieut-Col W Tanner
A Coy Capt D Heenan
B Coy Capt E Barlow
C Coy Capt W Gray
D Coy Border Major H Gee

3rd Battalion Transvaal & Rhodesia Lieut-Col E F Thackeray
A Coy Capt E Vivian
B Coy Wit Rifles Capt R Medlicott MC
C Coy Rand Light Inf Capt J Jackson
D Coy Capt L Tomlinson

4th Battalion SA Scottish Lieut-Col F A Jones DSO (Major D MacLeod DCM)
A Coy Cape Town Hldrs Capt S Russell
B Coy 1st Tvl Scottish Capt T Ross (Major D R Hunt)
C Coy 2nd Tvl Scottish Capt G Marshall
D Coy Natal & Caledonians Capt E Clerk

Appendix VII

Decorations and Mentions

VC – Victoria Cross

Pte W F Faulds

CB – Companion of the Bath
Brig-Gen H T Lukin

CMG – Companion (of the Order) of St Michael and St George
Lieut-Col W Dawson
Lieut-Col F A Jones DSO (posthumous)

DSO – Distinguished Service Order
Major M S Power
Lieut-Col W E C Tanner
Lieut-Col E F Thackeray
Captain L W Tomlinson

A Victoria Cross.
(I Uys)

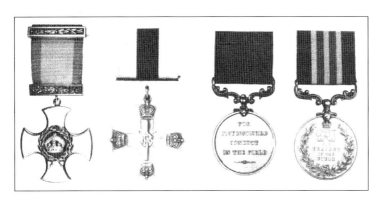

The Distinguished Service Order, Military Cross, Distinguished Conduct Medal,
Military Medal. (Joslin)

MC – Military Cross
Captain H W M Bamford
Captain M B Lawrie SAMC
Captain S Liebson
Captain A W M MacDonald
Captain T H Ross
Captain S W E Style
Captain E V Vivian
Captain T Welsh
Lieut L Greene
Lieut J L Shenton
Lieut W Thorburn
Sec-Lieut F W S Burton
Sec-Lieut C O Connock
Sec-Lieut F H English
Sec-Lieut G G Green
Sec-Lieut E J Phillips
CSM J Wilson

DCM – Distinguished Conduct Medal
A/RSM E E Pebble
A/CSM J M Thomson
S/Sergeant L H Welsh SAMC
Sergeant G E Marshall
Sergeant J Naisby
L/Corporal W H Shapcott
Private W M Healy
Private A J Loubser
Private G G Tanner
Private N J Vlok

MM – Military Medal
Sergeant W S McDonald
Corporal H L Sumner
Corporal G W Williams
L/Corporal W N Flanagan
L/Corporal F L Garland
L/Corporal J Hall
L/Corporal G A Hort
L/Corporal G C Strickland
Private V W Allen
Private G F Baker
Private G T Baker

Private S Dunstone
Private A Estment
Private J L Granger
Private W F Harris
Private T H Holiday
Private W Hollingberry
Private E E Hollington
Private R J Holmes
Private F G Moneron
Private W Prentice
Private M Smuts
Private W A Stewart
Private H M Taylor
Private G Thomas

Mentioned in Despatches

Four attributions

Lieut Walter James Hill (2nd Bn B Coy) Killed.
Recommended for the VC by Lieut-Col W E C Tanner but was awarded a Mention in Despatches (at the time, besides the VC, it was the only posthumous award permitted).
Sergeant D Schurray 4th Bn Recommended for the MM but was awarded Mention in Despatches.
Private Richard James Holmes Brigade Headquarters Wounded 19 July Awarded Military Medal
Private Marcel Raffard Smuts Brigade Headquarters Awarded Military Medal

57 Recommendations

1st SAI Battalion

Sergeant Stokill
Corporal Louis Leonard Aarons Wounded
Corporal G E Dunn
Private Allan S Montgomery Wounded 19 July
Private W J Ravenscroft
Private Arnold Sharp
Private W H Williams

2nd SAI Battalion

Sec-Lieut Garnet George Green Wounded Awarded MC
Lance-Cpl A L Kelly
Private John A Brook

Private D C Ratcliffe
Private J H Rubenson

3rd SAI Battalion
Sec-Lieut A E Sharpe Wounded 20 July
Corporal Henry John Hunter
Corporal George Watkin Williams
Lance-Cpl Robert Pinnock Wounded 16 July
Lance-Cpl Gerald C Strickland
Private C W Arnot Wounded 15 July
Private Richard Beland
Private Frank Bird Wounded
Private Howard Godfrey Capel Killed 19 July
Private Alfred Abraham Davis
Private William Henry Felton
Private Cyril Rosser Giles
Private Ralph Eric Harris Killed 19 July
Private Wesley N F Humphrey Wounded 18 July
Private Vincent John Kelly Wounded
Private Peter Knox
Private George Truscott Lobb Wounded 19 July
Private Charles Ernest Long
Private W Moloney
Private John Ernest T Noble
Private Henry John Norton
Private Denis O'Keefe
Private Henry Edward Osmond
Private William Preston
Private John Starrs Wounded
Private B Thompson
Private Joseph Henry Trewatha Wounded 15 July
Private Marinus A K van Holst
Private William Wilcocks
Drummer H Cooper

4th SAI Battalion
Lieut Arthur Hugh Brown Killed 16 July
Corporal Horace Lawrence Sumner
Lance-Cpl T C Butler
Lance-Cpl John Hall
Lance-Cpl Donald Hogarth
Private Dirk J du Toit
Private Hubert Jacob Margolis

Private James McPherson
Private Andrew F Morgan
Private John E Neilson
Private John B Rossiter
Private W S Simpson
Private Charles Stanley Slade
Private Edward C Thompson
Private William Hubert Thompson

(Above extracted from the Delville Wood website and 'Rollcall – the Delville Wood Story)

OBE – Order of the British Empire
Captain R F C Medlicott MC (3rd Bn B Coy)

Montenegrin Order of Danilo
Captain R F C Medlicott MC (3rd Bn B Coy)

Montenegrin Silver Medal for Merit
Sergeant J Naisby (3rd Bn D Coy)
Private R H Morgan (4th Bn C Coy)

Bibliography

English-language sources

Alhadeff, Vic, *South Africa in two World Wars* (1979) Don Nelson, Cape Town.

Anon., Deeds that Thrill the Empire (1920) Hutchison, London.

Buchan, J, *The History of the South African Forces in France* (1920) Thomas Nelson, London.

Carstens, J.A., *Fortune Through My Fingers* (1962) Howard Timmins.

Cave, Nigel, *Battleground Europe – Delville Wood* (1999) Leo Cooper, Pen & Sword Books Ltd, Barnsley.

Cornwell, Richard, *Militaria* 7/2 1977.

Couzens, Tim, *The Great Silence* (2014) Art Publishers (Pty) Ltd and Times Media (Pty) Ltd.

Crys-Williams, Jennifer, *South African Despatches* (1989) Ashanti Publishers, Johannesburg.

Digby, Peter, *Pyramids and Poppies* (1993) Ashanti Publishing (Pty) Ltd, Rivonia.

Farrar-Hockley, A.H., *The Somme* (1964) B T Batsford Ltd.

Genis, G, Delville Wood: Eighty Years (1996*) Militaria* Vol 26(1).

Liddel-Hart, Captain A H, *History of the First World War* (1970) Cassell & Co.

Lukin, Gen H.T., His scrapbook – A701 at Cape Archives.

Nash, David (ed), *German Army Handbook, April 1918* (Arms & Armour Press) (1977) London.

Militaria 8/3 1978 re Pte A.J. Loubser.

South African Military History Journal: June 2011 re A. R. Knibbs.

Schoeman, Chris, *The Somme Chronicles – South Africans on the Western Front* (2014) Zebra Press, Randomstruik, Cape Town.

Smith, Gordon's Letters, Edited by Emile Badenhorst of the Port Elizabeth Bayworld Museum.

Standard Encyclopaedia of South Africa. Nasou Ltd.

Sutton, Joan & Kantey, Mike, *Touching Circles* (2009) the Watermark Press, Plettenberg Bay.

'The Story of Delville Wood – Told in Letters from the Front'. *Cape Times*.

The War Illustrated.

Uys, Ian, *Delville Wood* (1983) Uys Publishers, Johannesburg.

Uys, Ian, *Longueval* (1986) Uys Publishers, Germiston.

Uys, Ian, *Rollcall: The Delville Wood Story* (1991) Uys Publishers, Germiston.

Uys, Ian, *Devil's Wood* (2006) Fortress Books, Knysna.

Whitte, Tyler, *The Last Kaiser* (1977) William Heinemann, London.

Williams, Alpheus F., *Some Dreams come True* (1948) Howard Timmins, Cape Town.

German-language sources

Amtliche Kriegsdepeschen für Juli 1916.

Anspach, Siegfried, Hauptmann (Regt Adj of RIR 107) & Flach, Dr Erhard, Oblt dR(Bn Adj RIR 107) *Das Königlich Sächsische Reserve-Infanterie-Regiment Nr 107* (Wilhelm & Bertha Baensch Stiftung) (1927) Dresden.

Brennfleck, Major Joseph Karl (retd), *Das Königlich Bayerische 16 Infanterie–Regiment Grossherzog Ferdinand von Toskana* [Grand Duke Ferdinand of Toskana – Bavarian patron], Bavarian Kriegsarchiv (1931).

Bamberg, Georg, *Das Königlich Sächsische Reserve-Infanterie-Regiment Nr 106* (Wilhelm & Bertha von Baensch Stiftung) (1925) Dresden.

Bilder aus der Sommeschlacht.

Extract from a diary … of a German soldier of the 3rd Company, I Bn 153 Regt, 8th Div, among Gen W.E.C. Tanner's papers.

Von Falkenhayn, Erich, General dI, *Die Oberste Heeresleitung 1914-1916 in ihren wichtigsten Entschließungen* (1920) Ernst Siegfried Mittler & Son) Berlin.

Von Gallwitz, Max, Artillery General (retd), *Erleben im Westen* (1932) E S Mittler & Sohn, Berlin.

Gruson, Oberst Ernst, *Das Königlich Preussische 4 Thüringische Infanterie-Regiment Nr 72* (1930) Gerh Stalling Oldenburg i.O.

Heintz, Dr Hans Oblt dR, *Das Königlich Sächsische Reserve-Infanterie-Regiment Nr 133.*

Keil, Hermann, Major dR & Von Littrow, Carl Edler, Hauptmann dR, *Das Königlich Sächsische Reserve-Jäger-Batallion No 13* (Wilhelm & Bertha von Baensch Stiftung) (1934) Dresden.

Moeller, Hanns, Fritz von Below, General der Infanterie. In 'Generals of the Great War' series (1939) Bernhard & Graefe, Berlin.

Mueller, P Major; von Fabeck, Oberst & Riesel, Oberstlt. *Geschichte des Reserve-Infanterie-Regiments Nr.99* (Bernhard Sporn) Zeulenroda, (1936) Thüringen.

Von Muelmann, Oberst aD and Mohs, Oblt aD, *Geschichte des Lehr-Infanterie-Regiments und seiner Stammformationen im Auftr. des Reichsverbandes der Lehr-Infanterie nach den amtlichen Kriegstagebüchern und persönlichen Aufzeichnungen* (1935) Bernhard Sporn Zeulenrode, Thüringen.

Reymann, Major Martin R, *Das Infanterie-Regiment von Alvensleben (6 Brandenburgische) Nr 52 im Weltkriege 1914-1918* (1926) Gerh Stalling Oldenburg iO.

Ritter, Holger Oberstleutnant (retd), *Schleswig-Holsteinisches Infanterie Regiment Nr 163* (1926) Gerh Stalling Oldenburg i.O.

Reichsarchiv, Albrecht von Stosch, Oberstlt, formerly of 8/153, *Schlachten des Weltkrieges Somme-Nord Band 20/21* (1927) Gerhard Stalling Oldenburg i.O.

Schmidt-Osswald, Ernst (Royal Prussian Major), *Das Altenburger Regiment 9 Thüringisches Infanterie-Regiment Nr 153* (1927) Gerhard Stalling Oldenburg i.O.

Von Schoenfeld, Major Ernst, *Das Grenadier-Regiment Prinz Karl von Preussen (2 Brandenburgisches) Nr 12* (1926) Gerhard Stalling Oldenburg i.O.

Von Vormann, Wolfgang (Kriegsleutnant), *Infanterie-Regiment Fürst Leopold von Anhalt – Dessau (1 Magdeburgisches) Nr 26* (1925-29, 6 vols) Gerh Stalling Oldenburg i.O.

Index

INDEX OF PLACES

Aberdeen, Cape, 109, 128
Aisne (River), 195, 197
Albert, 37, 50, 57, 67, 137, 182
Alsace, 121, 195
Altenburg, 38, 196
Amiens, 48-50
Ancre (River), 66-67, 195
Armentières, 51, 96
Arras, 172, 174, 179, 183, 185, 195-197
Austria, 40, 88

Bapaume, 67, 98, 100, 105
Bazentin le Grand, 53, 67, 81, 84, 87
Belgium, 38, 50, 180
Berlin, 87-88, 171, 177-178, 207
Bernafay Wood, 58, 62-65, 69, 96, 106, 114, 132, 142, 144, 167, 176-177
Bonn, 38, 88
Bordon Camp, 27, 29-30, 51, 69
Braune Stellung ('Brown line') trench postions, xiii, xix, 52, 66, 82, 87, 195
Brighton, 23, 183, 187
Buchanan Street, 113, 127, 130, 139, 150-151, 156, 189
Butte de Warlencourt , 172, 175, 178, 180-182, 184, 186-187

Cambrai, 67, 100, 186
Cape, the, xvii, 21, 23, 26-27, 44, 122, 175, 181, 185
Corbie 50, 170, 183

Delville Wood, i, xi-xiv, xvi, xviii-xix, 37, 52-54, 69, 71-72, 74-75, 77-78, 85-87, 89-91, 94-102, 104-105, 107, 110-112, 115-117, 119-121, 123-127, 131, 137, 140, 145-149, 156-159, 161-163, 165, 168-169, 172-173, 175-176, 178-183, 185-195, 205-207 (Devil's Wood 190, 207)
Denmark, 179, 197
Dresden, 88, 182, 207
Dulmen, 171, 181, 184
Durban, xii, 171, 184, 193

East London, 92, 96, 108, 177, 182
Eastern Province, 23, 107
Egypt, 30, 44, 51, 72, 176, 185, 188
England, ii, iv, 26, 40-41, 44-45, 169, 174, 177
Etineham Camp, 50-51

Fampoux, 172, 174-175, 177, 180
Flanders, 43, 198
Flers, viii, xx, 53-54, 69, 81, 85-86, 97-102, 105, 116, 118, 121, 127, 147, 157-158, 169, 195-196
Flers Road, 97, 99, 105
Foureaux Riegel, 53, 121
Foureaux Wood, 101, 121, 195

Gallipoli, 43, 188
Galway, Ireland, 183, 187
Gauche Wood, 173, 178

German South West Africa, xix, 29-30, 36, 74, 87
Germany, xvi, 38-39, 87, 179, 186, 196
Ginchy, 53, 85, 89, 99, 102-103, 115, 121, 125, 147-148, 195
Ginchy Road, 102-103, 147
Gouzeacourt, 172-173
Gueudecourt, 100, 104, 115
Guillemont, 53-54, 67, 87, 89, 120, 188-189

Halazin, 31, 153
Hampshire, 27, 178
High Wood, 53, 71, 100, 190
Hill 60, 195
Hill 140, 100, 104-105, 115

India, 23, 25, 175
Italy, 38, 40, 185

Johannesburg, 71, 112, 165, 175-178, 186, 206-207

Kimberley 23, 30, 44, 55, 107, 122, 144, 176, 178, 200
King William's Town, 28, 32, 145
Krugersdorp Hospital, 187

Le Bizet, 43, 47
Le Cateau, 173, 196-197
London, i, 27-29, 70, 92, 96, 108, 126, 169-170, 175, 177, 179, 181-183, 185, 206-207
Longueval, viii, x-xi, xiii-xv, xviii-xix, 37, 52-54, 69-77, 79-87, 89, 91, 96, 98-102, 104-107, 110, 112, 114, 117-118, 120-122, 125-126, 130-132, 135, 138, 142-145, 148, 150, 155, 157, 159-160, 163, 188-190, 195, 207
Loos, 43, 195-197

Mafeking, 25, 73
Mametz, 54, 173
Maricourt, 50-51, 83, 125
Marrières Wood, 173, 175-176, 178, 180, 184, 185

Marseilles, ix, 41-42, 163
Mersa Matruh, ix, 30-31, 33
Messines, 173, 175
Mons, 37, 196
Montauban, x, 52-53, 57, 59-60, 69-70, 74-75, 83, 122, 131, 150, 182

Natal, viii, 23-24, 26, 92, 97, 127, 161, 184, 187, 199-200

Passchendaele, 172, 174
Pietermaritzburg, viii, 23, 92, 184
Plymouth, 27, 30
Port Elizabeth, xvii, 73, 77, 109, 176, 181, 184, 206
Port Nolloth, 26, 175
Potchefstroom, 21, 26, 29, 181
Pozières, 53, 66-67, 178, 188, 190
Pretoria, xvi, 174
Princes Street, 92, 105, 111, 146, 157-158
Prussia, 38, 188

Queenstown, 131, 180

Richmond Hospital, London, 181, 183
Robertson, Western Cape, x, 50, 176
Rondebosch, 27, 42
Rouen, 170-171, 181-183
Russia, 38, 40, 176

Saxony, 38, 195
'Second Line', xix, 52, 66-67, 81, 190, 195
Somme region, i, x, xiii, xviii-xix, 37, 40, 47, 49-50, 52, 56, 64, 66-67, 87-88, 100-101, 157, 163, 167-168, 172, 181, 188, 195-198, 206, 208
South Africa, i-ii, x, xii, xvi, 61, 121, 154, 165, 169, 174-175, 178, 180-183, 185-186, 191-192, 206
Strand Street, 92, 112, 126, 134, 157
Strassburg, 121, 195
Sugar Factory, (Waterlot Farm), x, 53-54, 81, 85, 89, 101, 104, 112, 120-121, 195

Suzanne, 50, 59-60, 184

Thiepval, 52, 81, 165, 187, 196
'Third Line', 53, 121
Trônes Wood, xi, 54, 60, 62-63, 69, 87, 89, 119, 154, 182, 195

Uitenhage, ii, 73, 122, 125, 175

Verdun, 40, 52, 67, 117, 127, 165, 188

Waterlot Farm, x-xi, 53-54, 90, 104, 112, 119, 121, 139-140, 188
Western Province, 23, 26, 180
Ypres 37, 172, 174-176, 179, 183, 185, 195

Zabern, 121, 195

INDEX OF BRITISH AND IMPERIAL ARMY FORMATIONS

General
Royal Field Artillery 60, 179
Royal Flying Corps 174, 181, 183
South African Medical Corps (SAMC), 114, 142, 144, 152, 155, 202
SA Light Trench Mortar Battery 131, 135, 187

Armies
2nd Army 52, 198

Corps
III Corps 38, 198
XIII Corps, vi, 175, 198
XV Corps 182, 198

Divisions
3rd Division, 155, 160, 185, 198
9th (Scottish) Division vi, xiii, 43, 47, 65, 70-71,90, 155, 163, 172, 180, 198
18th Division, 65, 198

Brigades
1st (SA Infantry) Brigade, vii, 21, 90,91,200
26th Brigade, 71, 90, 106, 143, 145, 198
27th Brigade, 62, 71-72, 122, 148, 199
76th Brigade, 128, 146, 155

Regiments
Black Watch 43, 62, 74, 76, 78, 106, 143, 198
Dorset Yeomanry, 34, 36
Imperial Light Horse 25, 186

Kaffrarian Rifles 29, 96
Kimberley Regiment 107, 176
King's Own Scottish Borderers 122, 126, 143
Norfolk Regiment 150, 161
Royal Scots 34, 43, 72, 107, 110-111, 121-122, 199
Royal Welch Fusiliers xi, 159-161
Seaforth Highlanders 62, 71, 111, 154, 198
South African Scottish, ix, 25-26, 30, 41-42, 62, 64, 136, 199-200
Transvaal Scottish ix, 26, 41-42, 106
Witwatersrand Rifles 25, 123

Battalions
1st SAI Battalion, 23, 26, 30, 34-36, 42-44, 46, 55, 58, 60, 73-75, 77, 81, 91, 93-94, 97-98, 107-108, 110-111, 122, 124-126, 128-131, 133-134, 143-145, 154, 162, 165, 168, 174-176, 178-180, 182-184, 199-200
1st SAI Battalion HQ, 125, 130, 174-175
1st SAI Battalion M-G Coy, 94, 124, 129, 143, 154, 180
1st SAI Battalion, A Coy, 122, 134, 174-175
1st SAI Battalion, B Coy, 34, 43, 73, 77, 81, 91, 98, 107-108, 125, 128, 130-131, 133-134, 143, 165, 168, 176, 182, 184
1st SAI Battalion, C Coy, 30, 36, 44, 55, 122, 134, 144, 178-179

1st SAI Battalion, D Coy, 26, 35, 42, 44, 46, 55, 58, 60, 65, 75, 79, 91, 97, 131, 162, 175-176, 179, 183

2nd SAI Battalion, 24, 28, 29-30, 31-33, 47, 49, 51, 58, 62, 64, 71, 91-92, 95, 97-98, 106, 111-112, 114, 125, 127, 132, 134, 136, 139, 141, 150, 154, 159, 161-162, 171-172, 176-180, 184-186, 199-200, 203

2nd SAI Battalion HQ, 95, 106, 134, 162, 176, 185

2nd SAI Battalion B Coy, 49, 95, 112, 132, 203

2nd SAI Battalion C Coy, 136, 150, 154, 159, 178, 180, 184, 186

2nd SAI Battalion D Coy, 29-30, 32, 47, 51, 58, 71, 92, 97, 98, 114, 125, 134, 136, 177, 179, 185

3rd SAI Battalion, 25, 30, 64, 91, 92, 95, 98, 112, 124, 127-128, 131, 136, 139, 145, 150-153, 165,171,175, 179-181, 183, 186, 199-200, 205

3rd SAI Battalion HQ, 180, 186

3rd SAI Battalion, A Coy, 95, 124

3rd SAI Battalion, B Coy, 95, 136, 150, 152-153, 186, 205

3rd SAI Battalion, C Coy, 64, 112, 127, 139, 151, 165, 175, 179, 181

3rd SAI Battalion, D Coy, 95, 128, 152, 205

4th SAI Battalion, ix, 25,26, 30, 41, 61-63, 65, 90, 94, 95, 98, 105-107,112, 125, 126, 128, 136, 138, 145,150,155, 162, 172, 174, 178, 187, 199-200, 203- 205

4th SAI Battalion, A Coy, 63, 95, 107,136

4th SAI Battalion, C Coy, 41, 125, 138, 172, 174, 205

4th SAI Battalion, D Coy, 61, 95, 107,187

5th Cameron Highlanders, 90, 112, 198

6th King's Own Scottish, 122, 199

11th Royal Scots, 72, 107, 110-111, 121-122, 199

INDEX OF BRITISH AND IMPERIAL ARMY PERSONNEL

Allen, Percival (Percy) Joseph, 73, 78

Ashworth, Private Gwyn, 44, 55-57, 112, 130, 174

Baker, Private George Frederick, viii-ix, 23-24, 91, 108, 111, 172, 174, 202

Betteridge, Private Arthur H., xi, 41, 125, 138, 172, 174

Burges, Major Edward,   viii, 22, 78, 128, 131, 134-135, 200

Burton, Lieutenant F.W.S., ix, 24, 202

Carlson, Bill, 26, 80

Carstens, Private Jack, ix, 26-27, 35, 79, 91, 93, 131, 175, 206

Catton, Lance-Corporal Willie, 22, 122, 175

Churchill, Winston, 43, 52

Cockroft, Private Philip, 31-32

Congreve VC, Lieutenant-Gen William, 71, 155, 175, 198

Congreve, Major Billy, xi, 160

Cook, The Rev., 65, 125, 138

Cooper, Private/Drummer Henry (Harry), x, 64, 112-113, 127, 151, 175, 204, 206

Cristel, Maurice, xi, 162-163, 187

Croft, Lieutenant-Colonel William, 72, 110-111

Dawson, Lieutenant-Colonel Frederick Stuart, viii, 22-23, 73, 78, 89, 112, 123, 132, 135, 141, 144-145, 150, 171, 173, 175, 200-201

English, Lieutenant Frederick William Hawthorne, x, xvi, xviii-xix, 32, 43, 50, 67-68, 83, 107, 109-110, 118, 125, 134, 148, 157, 168, 176, 180, 196, 202, 206

Faulds, Private William Frederick, x, xii, 73, 108-109, 111, 121, 131, 172-173, 176, 201

Featherstone, Second-Lieutenant Clive, xi, 109, 128, 134, 176, 185

Fitz, Private Eddie H., 95-96, 106, 162, 176-177

Furse, Major-General W.T., vi, 71, 123, 198

Gee, Major Harry, 21, 111, 125, 127, 136

George V (King), 29, 171

Giddy, Private Walter, ix, xvii, 28-32, 41, 43, 47-48, 51, 58, 62-63, 71, 97, 114, 141, 167, 172, 177

Green, Second-Lieutenant Garnet G., xii, 139, 155, 159, 161, 167, 173, 176, 178, 202-203

Greene, Lieutenant L., viii, 23, 202

Greener, Private R., 171-172

Griffiths, Sergeant Stanley, 73, 125

Grimsdell, Private Robert 'Bob', 112, 178

Grindley, Private David, xvii, 144, 178

Haarhof, Second-Lieutenant Allan, 55-57, 112

Haig, General Sir Douglas, 71,198

Heal, Major, 42, 173

Hill, Private Albert, 160-161,

Hill, Captain Eustace St C., viii, x-xi, 23, 35-36, 74, 80, 92-93, 96-97, 100, 104-106, 110, 112-115, 125, 131-132, 136, 145, 155, 160-161, 178-179, 182, 195, 203

Hill, Padre Eustace, 106, 114, 125, 131, 136, 155, 182

Hill, Lieutenant Walter, x, 92-93, 112, 132

Hoptroff, Captain Wallace Frank, 134-137

Hunt, Major D.R., ix, 25, 65, 98, 106-107, 112, 150, 200

Hurlin, Sergeant John 'Charlie', 109-110

Jones, DSO, Lieutenant-Colonel Frank, ix, 25-26, 64-65, 200-201

Kirkman, family, viii, x, xii, xvii-xix, 77, 144, 179

Knibbs, Second-Lieutenant Arthur, xi-xii, 92, 134, 179

Larmuth, Lieutenant W., viii, 22, 58, 76-78

Lawrie, Captain, 142, 145

Lee, Lance Corporal Frederick Charles, 165, 179

Liebson, Captain/Dr. Stephen, xii, 127, 173, 175, 180

Liefeldt, Lieutenant A.W., viii-ix, 22, 31, 33-35, 66

Loubser, Private Albert Johannes, 137, 179-180, 202, 206

Lukin, Brigadier Henry Timson 'Tim',viii, 21, 34, 98, 122, 180, 199-200

Macleod, Major, 65, 128, 141, 150

Marillier, Private Frank, xi, 136, 154-155, 159, 168, 180

Marr, Private Albert, ii, ix, xi, 26, 34

Maskew, Private Frank, xi-xii, xvii, 36, 75, 94, 124, 129, 143, 154, 181

McDonald, Captain Albert, 172

Medlicott, Captain Richard, 136, 139, 150, 152, 154

Miller, Captain Allister M., viii, 22-23, 34, 50, 78, 106-107, 109, 125, 181, 200

Miller, Captain George, 50, 107

Naisby, Sergeant J., 202, 205

Nash, Private James Yeatman 'Boysie', x, xvii, 77, 107, 130, 206

Nicholson, Second-Lieutenant C.F, viii, 22, 27, 46, 125

O'Keefe, Private Dennis, 63, 204

Oldfield, Private Henry, 96, 106

Orpen, Sir William, xii, 193

Pattison, Lance Corporal Charles Joseph, x, xii, xvii, 73-74, 77, 81, 91, 107, 130, 143, 154, 165, 168, 172, 182

Philips, Lieutenant Edward, vi, ix, xii, 24,125,131,135, 156,159,161 172, 182,202

Proctor VC, Captain Andrew, 174, 181

Reid, Lt. Chauncey, ix, 26, 29, 32, 41, 45, 47, 58, 60, 65, 75, 80, 170

Roe, Fatty, 60, 63

Samuels, Private Joseph, xii, 95, 183-184

Shenton, Lieutenant J.L., ix, 25, 202

Smith, Private Gordon, xii, xvii, 43-44, 77, 91, 110, 132, 135, 173, 184, 206

Stuart, Private Charles 'Charlie' B., 150, 184

Stuckey, Lieutenant Alfred Jeremiah, xi, 134, 176, 185

Style, Lieutenant Sydney, viii, 22, 28, 125, 145, 202

Sumner, Corporal Sam, 136, 162

Tanner, Lieutenant-Colonel William E.C., viii, xi-xii, xvi, 23-24, 29, 93, 95-96, 105, 112, 123, 125-127, 161, 173, 185-186, 200-203, 207

Tatham, Second-Lieutenant Errol, viii, 23, 92, 134

Thackeray, Lieutenant-Colonel Edward Frank vi, ix, xvi, 24-25, 123-124, 127, 144-145, 150-152, 155-156, 159-161, 166, 186, 200-201

Thompson, Private Bob, 65, 72

Thomson, Acting Company Sergeant Major James ix, 22, 25, 139, 186, 202

Walshe, Chaplain/Captain C.J., viii, 23

Weldon, Private Cyril, ix, xvii,27, 44, 55, 97, 169-170, 204

Wepener, Private Victor, xi, 153, 186

Woolf, Lance- Corporal Maurice, ix, 30, 37, 47

Young VC, Lieutenant Alexander 'Sandy', ix, xii, xiv, 21, 24-25, 61, 95, 127, 151, 166, 168, 172, 184, 187, 191

INDEX OF GERMAN ARMY FORMATIONS

Armies

1st Army, (von Below), 52, 87

Divisions

8th Division, 87, 99, 100, 105, 207

10th (Bavarian) Division, 66, 103

12th (Reserve) Division, 87, 99, 195

Regiments

GR 12, 164

IR 16, 85, 87, 89

IR 23, 99

IR 26 x-xi, 26, 85-87, 89, 100-102, 105, 115, 117, 120-121, 148, 157, 164, 177

IR 38, 99

IR 52 148, 156-159

IR 53, 117

IR 72, 67, 98, 100, 102-103, 105, 117, 119, 128, 146, 158-159, 197

IR 153, 98, 100, 103-105, 114, 117-118, 120-121, 127, 136, 146, 156-157, 159, 196

IR 163 (Holsteiners), 98, 117

IR 178, 195

IR 182, 195

RIR 99, 81, 121, 195

RIR 104, 127, 146

RIR 106, 104, 195

RIR 107, x, 87-89, 95, 98-100, 103-105, 120, 127, 159, 186, 195, 207

INDEX OF GERMAN ARMY PERSONNEL

Armin, General Friedrich Sixt von 66, 100

Bieler, Hauptmann, 115, 146

Falkenhayn, General Erich von, 37, 40, 86

Gallwitz, General Max von, 52, 207
Grautoff, Oberst Paul, x, xix, 87, 101, 105, 157, 164, 177

Huber, Hauptmann, 101, 103

Killermann, Major, 82-85
Könemann, Oberstleutnant, 105, 157

Ludwig, Oberst Karl Adam, x, 88, 98, 127, 136, 186

Noack, Leutnant Anno Ludwig, x, 85-86, 182

Rausch, Hauptmann, 101, 117, 120, 121

Schönberg, Major, xi, 148-149
Stosch, Major von, 100, 115, 117

Weber, Oberleutnant dR, 82-83, 157
Wuthenau Oberst Graf Karl Adam Ludwig von, x, 88, 98, 104, 127, 136, 186, 195

INDEX OF GENERAL & MISCELLANEOUS TERMS

Aid Post 125, 142, 144-145
Altenburgers, 100, 114, 120, 127, 146, 156-157, 196
Armistice 172-173, 183, 186

Boer War, 21-22, 63, 136, 139, 171, 185
Boers, i, 21-22, 63, 92, 128, 136, 139, 153, 171, 185, 194
Botha, State President, Mr P W, 169, 186
Brandenburgers, 148, 156-158, 188, 191

CMG medal, viii, 21, 176, 185-186, 200-201

DCM medal, i, ix, xii, 25-26, 65, 126, 179, 185-186, 200, 202
DSO medal, viii-ix, xi, 21-22, 25-26, 72, 153, 155, 160, 176, 181, 185-186, 200-201

Eastern Front, 52, 186

German Official History, 82, 146

Grave locations and site, 77, 120, 123, 168, 173, 192

Iron Cross medal, ix, 39, 182, 187

Jackie the baboon, (mascot), 26, 34

Knight's Cross medal, 177, 186

Legion of Honour medal, 61, 175, 187

Pasha, Gaafer, 30, 36

Red Cross 32, 175, 185

SS *Dunvegan Castle*, ix, 26-27
SS *Oriana*, ix, 30, 37
Saxons 95, 136, 144, 146, 157, 188
Senussi Arabs, ix, 30-31, 36
Somme (Battle of), 64, 163, 168, 188
South African Railways, 174, 184
South African War, 21, 23-26, 29-30, 36, 107, 122, 128, 155
Springboks 43, 124, 130, 133, 191, 194